THE BOGTROTTER'S GUIDE

Chris Holmes

Published by Sigma Leisure - an imprint of
Sigma Press, 1 South Oak Lane, Wilmslow, Cheshire SK9 6AR, England.

British Library Cataloguing in Publication Data
A CIP record for this book is available from the British Library.

ISBN: 1-85058-401-X

Typesetting and Design by: Sigma Press, Wilmslow, Cheshire.

Cover design: Design House

Printed by: J.W. Arrowsmith Ltd, Bristol.

Disclaimer: the information in this book is given in good faith and is believed to be correct at the time of publication. No responsibility is accepted by either the author or publisher for errors or omissions, or for any loss or injury howsoever caused. You must judge your own fitness, competence and experience.

PREFACE

THE upland moors of the Dark Peak have acquired something of a sinister reputation, over time. Visitors to the Peak National Park Information Centre at Fieldhead, Edale, are warned that Kinder Scout is on the same latitude as Labrador and Siberia. The late Alfred Wainwright, author of the unique *Pennine Way Companion*, reminds us that men have died on Bleaklow. Do high-level walkers harbour a death-wish?

When the Pennine moors turn to white under severe winter conditions, and self-styled 'experts', from weather forecasters to newspaper columnists, berate those selfish and wholly irresponsible individuals who venture onto the high ground for endangering not only their own lives but those of Mountain Rescue Volunteers, should the responsible rambler and climber restrict his or her activities to the gentler dales, and shun the notoriously bleak moorland plateaux?

The Dark Peak Moors most certainly demand respect; only a fool will underestimate them, whatever the time of year. Yet, there is little justification for fear. Although some areas might instill a feeling of apprehension and intimidation, the real dangers need to be put into perspective. With a thorough knowledge of navigation techniques, combined with sensible clothing and a reasonable degree of fitness, even the most desolate regions can be explored at any season.

This book is intended to encourage readers to experience the wildest parts of the beautiful Peak National Park, and to seek out and find the vital places where personal rediscovery is still possible.

The suggested routes have been selected to introduce ramblers to a variety of scenery and terrain. The directions and sketch maps must be used in conjunction with the Ordnance Survey Outdoor Leisure Map *The Dark Peak* (1:25000). A compass, preferably of the *Silva* type, is essential on many of the walks. Navigation begins with good planning, and a few moments spent with the map learning the position of the main valleys and ridges opens up a range of possibilities: in open country, existing paths can be ignored and the pioneering spirit freely indulged.

It should be emphasised that the following routes are not immutable, or written in stone. Follow some of the dotted lines in the book; but it is far more satisfying to wander at will over this remarkable semi-wilderness. For this is what the art of bogtrotting is all about: a rare feeling of wide open space and freedom. Is there a better antidote to the artifice of the age?

Special thanks are due to the following:

Ron Collier, aviation historian and author of 'Dark Peak Aircraft Wrecks' (Vols. 1&2) ;

Roni Wilkinson, of Pen & Sword Books Ltd., publishers of the above;

Paul Harrop, who supplied photographs and transport;

Van 'The Man' Morrison, for providing inspiration;

And, most importantly, to Susan, for her constant support on and off the hill.

Chris Holmes

CONTENTS

Section B:
BOGTROTTING DELIGHTS

SECTION C:
BACKGROUND FOR BOGTROTTERS

SECTION A:

BOGTROTTING BASICS

1

THE PEAK LANDSCAPE

THE Peak National Park lies at the southern end of the Pennines – the backbone of England – and is divided into two distinct regions defined by geology: the White Peak, a rolling plateau of Carboniferous limestone riven by water-scoured dales; and the Dark Peak, which comprises the northern landscape of heather (ling) moorland and high, peat-laden plateaux intersected by valleys and bounded to the east by an almost continuous escarpment, the gritstone edges, great lines of grey rock severing the earth and dominating the skyline from Ladybower Reservoir in the Upper Derwent Valley to Chatsworth in the south. The rugged Dark Peak forms a horseshoe of millstone grit embracing the gentle White Peak, and the whole provides a fascinating area with diversity at the core of its appeal.

The Peak Park is a place of great natural beauty and a vital part of our heritage, but it is not "The Peak Experience", Arcadia free from conflict, with the countryside as a spurious representation of itself; here, nature reflects a wider reality, with strands of continuity and change intertwined.

Man and environment have interacted in the Peak throughout history and human activity has played and continues to play a central role in the creation and maintenance of the landscape; not least of all on the high-level 'wilderness' of the peat-blanketed gritstone plateaux.

EARLY RESIDENTS

Evidence of Palaeolithic man has been found in the limestone caves of the White Peak, and later nomadic subsistence hunters of the Mesolithic age began to settle throughout the Peak as widespread climatic changes encouraged the spread of forests; but the early hunters left no definite stamp on the landscape.

During the pre-Boreal period of the post-glacial years 10,000 years ago juniper, dwarf birch and willow colonised the tundras of northern Britain. Over the next 2,000 years of the Boreal period milder conditions meant a proliferation of Scots pine, birch, willow and hazel. The Atlantic period which followed provided even warmer, humid conditions, encouraging the growth of deciduous trees; this period, 7,500 to 5,000 years ago, introduced an era of stable growth for forests. With warmer weather human settlement increased in the Peak and the process of forest clearance began. The clearances increased grazing areas, initially for the hunters' quarry and later for domestic animals as the first farmers of the Neolithic age began to practise livestock and arable farming where conditions allowed.

Neolithic and early Bronze Age man thus initiated the process of shaping the land, and during this sub-Boreal period 5,000 to 2,500 years ago extensive burning and felling of the virgin forests, combined with intensive grazing, led to peat mosses and hardy plants replacing grassland in regions of nutrient-poor, acidic soils.

The people of the Bronze Age – often known as the Beaker or Food Vessel Peoples, after the artifacts unearthed by archaeologists – expanded their settlements from the fertile limestone plateau of the White Peak to the gritstone upland of the Dark Peak: Gib Hill, near the mysterious Neolithic limestone circle of Arbor Low, is one of many White Peak barrows or burial mounds belonging to the Bronze Age; whilst the Nine Ladies gritstone circle on Stanton Moor and the settlement earthworks above Curbar and Froggatt Edges at Bar Brook and Big Moor have provided a valuable insight into the lives of the Bronze Age settlers in the gritstone area. (The gritstone moors, relatively undisturbed by modern farming, continue to yield long-buried secrets. In 1992, a detailed survey at Gardom's Edge, near Bar Brook, revealed the remains of prehistoric fields and the sites of timber houses. Most spectacularly, excavations on the Edge led to the discovery of a huge prehistoric fort; the first of its kind to be found in Britain.)

The sub-Atlantic period, 2,500 years ago to the present day, brought wetter and cooler weather, and peat bogs spread as light, acidic soils became waterlogged. Broad-leaved woods – particularly oak, elm, ash, lime and hazel – became the dominant woodland throughout Britain.

Relatively little is known of the late Bronze/early Iron Age people who settled in the Peak during this sub-Atlantic period, but excavations of their numerous hill forts have indicated a lengthy occupation of the gritstone area. The largest, and archaeologically most important, of the Peak hill forts is the site crowning the summit of Mam Tor, overlooking the Hope Valley. (In the summer of 1993, Mam Tor was the subject of a high-profile conservation exercise as some 300 tons of materials were airlifted by helicopter onto the summit, as part of a bid to stop the extensive erosion caused by walkers; archaeology experts worked alongside National Trust workers during the critical stages, which involved laying stones no more than nine inches deep. Erosion and destruction of surface vegetation in vulnerable areas is the hills' natural response to heavy recreational use, and intensive regeneration work, from re-seeding with hardy grasses to the laying of stones or geo-textile mats is a costly enterprise; but the most expensive option of all is neglect, and vigilance is the price of the hills' survival so that future generations may have the opportunity to experience the natural beauty of the Peak.)

The Romans invaded the Peak around 7 AD, and built what was probably the central control fort of the area at Brough, in the Hope Valley. This fort, Navio, may have provided a defence against the indigent Brigantes who, it is not unreasonable to assume, resisted the imposition of martial law by the Mediterranean interlopers. There is, however, evidence that a peaceful settlement grew around Navio, and other civilian settlements from the period were established near Chee Dale and at Roystone Grange, Ballidon, where the remains of a farmstead and field systems have been identified.

The Peak provided a vital source of lead for the Romans, and it is known that mines were in operation throughout the occupation. The economic importance of the area justified the establishment of a cordon of forts manned by auxiliary units as part of a control system. Navio was linked to the fort at Glossop, Ardotalia (Melandra Castle), by the road familiar to latter-day travellers as Doctor's Gate: a mediaeval packhorse route later followed the original course of the Roman road and, apocryphal tales aside, this path is said to owe its name to Doctor John Talbot, vicar of Glossop between 1494 and 1550.

The Saturnalian Romans, placed in a landscape and climate more suited to the Stoic temperament, found a little relief in the warm spring waters of Aquae Arnemetiae (Buxton), connected to Navio by the road known as Batham Gate.

The colonial troops of the Roman Empire gradually departed from the Peak in the early 5th century, and the enigmatic era known as the Dark Ages began. Myth and legend abounds, but historians have discovered little hard evidence from this period; although some clues may be derived from place-names given by the British prior to the Anglo-Saxon invasion: Derwent, for example, comes from the British 'derva', meaning oak.

With the invasion and subsequent settlement of the Anglo-Saxons the roots of many modern villages were established, initially along the river valleys and later spreading to the high ground. The Anglo-Saxons were adept at carpentry, and their demand for wood as a building material meant that woodland continued to be cleared, creating further grazing land for livestock.

It was during Anglo-Saxon times that the first known references to the 'Peak' occur: a 7th century Charter, the Tribal Hidage, refers to the Pecsaetan, a local tribe of 'hill-dwellers', the name deriving from the ancient 'peac', meaning hill, and 'saetan' (or 'saetna'), meaning 'dwellers of'. The Peak, then, owes nothing to Doctor Johnson's dictionary definition of a peak as a "sharply pointed hill", and pedantic souls who bemoan the lack of 'true' peaks in the region (always excepting the limestone summits of Parkhouse and Chrome Hills, near Hollinsclough) should not be disappointed to find a series of plateaux and rounded hills throughout the Peak National Park.

By the mid-7th century, Christianity became the dominant religion. Early preaching crosses from the Saxon period, richly decorated with scrolls, still stand in the Peak, with particularly fine examples in the churchyards of Hope, Eyam and Bakewell; indeed, the parish church of All Saints, Bakewell, stands on the original site of a Saxon church.

The pagan Danes came to Anglian Mercia in the 9th century, and sacked the capital and main religious centre of Repton, destroying the monastery along with other tangible evidence of the Christian faith here and throughout Mercia. Following this period of violent disruption the Danes began to settle, and were eventually converted to Christianity.

By 1066 and the Norman Invasion, the colonisation of Christian England was complete. The Normans introduced a feudal system, and the Domesday Commissioners collected the necessary documentation. Many villages of the Peak were already well established by this time, although some areas were described in the Domesday Book as 'waste': under the Forest Laws,

Royal Forests were claimed and kept outside of the Common Law, to be preserved as a highly exclusive hunting ground for the rich and royal. This early example of the arbitrary removal of rights was applied to stretches of open country, cleared of trees during the preceding centuries, as well as to the remaining woodland. The Royal Forest of the High Peak was policed from Peveril Castle, the ruins of which still stand high above the village of Castleton. The castle was given to William Peveril, Keeper of the Royal Forest and bastard son of William the Conqueror, and this glorified hunting lodge declined in importance as the forests were reduced by the growing demand for building materials and fuel, and an increase in pasturing animals led to further clearances.

Farming developed throughout the Middle Ages, with a particular emphasis on sheep-grazing; it now became necessary to manage existing woodland by coppicing and selective felling to ensure a plentiful supply of essential timber.

Coppicing techniques were widely employed up to the 19th century, when coal replaced firewood as a major fuel source. Small scale forestry plantations, managed by coppicing, had become established during the 17th century. These early plantations were of deciduous trees, but conifers were eventually introduced. (The extensive afforestation of upland Britain is, however, a 20th century phenomenon, with massed-ranks of alien conifers obliterating scenery and destroying wildlife habitat whilst providing an investment, gilt-edged from date of issue, for high-income earners intent on mitigating their tax bills.)

Forestry management has had a massive impact on the environment, but perhaps the most significant development in the formation of the modern Peak landscape came with the Enclosure Movement and the Enclosure Acts of the 18th and 19th centuries, when land was parcelled up and 'acquired' by landlords: as land was enclosed – usurping the rights of peasants and smallholders, who often depended on common grazing – the moors were extended at the expense of the commoners, who were forced out of their agricultural homes and into the new towns to become industrial workers.

The management of heather moorland for grouse shooting dates back to the last century, when open access rights were effectively abolished (the traditional right to roam over Kinder Scout was repealed circa 1832) despite the fact that passage over the moors had been allowed for centuries; moreover, paths could be closed at the landowner's whim. The Enclosures not only altered the physical landscape; the various Acts helped in the creation of a new set of social relations, setting the stage for conflicts which continue to the present day.

The author on Black Hill (Paul Harrop)

MOORLAND MANAGEMENT

The Dark Peak moors are characterised by their openness and bleakness, yet life is there. This semi-wilderness is of great importance to the overall environment. The loss of moorland and attendant peat bogs on a national level, due to afforestation and agricultural developments has had serious consequences for bird, insect and plant life. According to the Council for the Protection of Rural England the amount of moorland (rough grazing land) in England has fallen by 440,000 hectares in the last 45 years; equivalent to a loss of 25% of the total. The Royal Society for the Protection of Birds attribute the decline of several species to habitat loss; the merlin, Britain's smallest raptor (diurnal bird of prey), has particularly suffered from huge loss of moorland in mid-Wales. The delightful golden plover, an upland breeding wader, has also declined, in the Peak as elsewhere. Clearly, it is not only the red grouse – the sportsman's quarry – that benefits from a moorland environment. The British Field Sports Society argue that without the sporting shotgun heather moorlands would be afforested or lost to useless bracken. Landowners have consistently claimed to be conservationists, concerned with the maintenance of a fragile eco-system and the preservation of a uniquely wild and beautiful landscape.

Productive grouse moor management requires a regular programme of controlled heather burning to ensure a plentiful supply of young, green shoots, on which the red grouse thrives. If the heather (or ling) plants grow beyond 10-15 years, production of food for the birds declines and as the bushes grow higher so the younger grouse and chicks have difficulty in reaching the shoots which grow at the tips. Careful burning destroys old shoots without damaging the actual roots of the heather. By the practice of rotational burning in strips, different heights of growth are created within a relatively small area; thus the moor carries heather of varying maturity: the younger, shorter heather providing essential green shoots and the older, taller heather providing the dense cover favoured by the red grouse for nesting sites.

The conditions that maintain large grouse populations are the very same that support a wide range of wildlife. At the same time as undoubtedly enhancing the environment, a properly managed grouse moor can maintain a rural economy. Bad management, adverse weather conditions, diseases caused by parasitic worms, all can decimate the grouse population and create a drop in employment and income, not only for gamekeepers and beaters, but also for hotels, field sports outfitters and seasonal workers. Unfortunately, some gamekeepers continue to blame birds of prey for any reduction in grouse numbers, and unjustifiable persecution of rare raptors still occurs, undermining the 'conservationist' stance of moorland owners.

Hen harriers, protected by law since 1954, are amongst the species regularly persecuted, although it has never been established that the species have any real effect on grouse populations; indeed, many gamekeepers believe that the impact of raptors on a moor is negligible. Nevertheless, some game rearers and moorland managers continue to shoot and poison rare birds as part of their policy of 'predator control'. The lives of protected birds are claimed each year by poisoned baits, including lumps of bread, hens' eggs and pegged-out rabbits, laced with pesticides which may have been approved for crop protection, but most certainly not for killing wild-life. Legislation, public opinion and education has helped to encourage a more sensitive approach where it is needed, and the attitude of many landowners and their employees is becoming more enlightened. It is now widely accepted that the few grouse taken by raptors means that a few less of the weakest game birds which have failed to secure territory and have therefore been banished to the relatively barren margins of the moor – where they are more easily picked-off by quartering birds of prey – will die of starvation during the harsh moorland winter. In the few cases where a shoot has been ruined by raptors driving grouse away under duress (some-times for a mile or more) the grouse have almost inevitably returned, being effectively 'tethered' to the moor by their diet. The possible loss of a day's sport cannot be used as a justification for the continuing persecution of some of Britain's rarest and most spectacular birds.

A recent development which has caused concern to many conservation-ists is the bulldozing of tracks, built to enable the ladies and gentlemen who shoot the moors to drive to the grouse butts. The tradition of the "long walk-in" appears to have been abandoned in favour of these landscape-scarring driveways. Ironically, two of the main reasons given by land-owners to explain their resistance to access proposals are that ramblers and climbers disturb wildlife and that the passage of boots over moorland causes unsightly erosion, particularly on peaty slopes, which have a far lower carrying capacity than level, dry grassland.

Although field sports and public access co-exist in many moorland areas, there are still vast places of uncultivated land where walkers have no right to tread. The freedom to roam remains an elusive goal for ramblers and climbers in the Peak National Park as elsewhere.

2

THE FREEDOM TO ROAM

THE Peak has drawn visitors for centuries, yet descriptive commentary of the area – particularly the high gritstone moors – has often been characterised by negative qualities: "desolate, wild and abandoned" wrote Defoe in 1726, "a howling wilderness". The Victorian visionary John Ruskin, whilst fulsome in his praise for the dales, dismissed the moors as "wholly without interest". Even modern writers, including the highly respected John Hillaby and Alfred Wainwright, have often been less than generous to the peaty plateaux of the Dark Peak.

Admiration for these fierce places denuded of ornament is a fairly recent notion; but contemporary thought has deep roots. The search for an Arcadian idyll, which can be traced back to Classical Greece, was highly popular in Elizabethan England, where idealised nature reflected moral beauty. In the mid-17th century, Rousseau sought to be "at one" with nature, to be totally absorbed in a "sensuous reverie". The cult of sensibility, the new religion of Nature and Truth embraced by the Romantic poets, including Wordsworth and Coleridge, who looked at nature in the high, mystical manner, has influenced latter-day responses to the countryside to some degree.

EARLY TOURISTS

Many early tourists were attracted to the Peak by 'The Seven Wonders' listed in Thomas Hobbes' book *De Mirabilibus Pecci* ('Of the Wonders of the Peak'),published in 1636. Hobbes, (whose later *Leviathan* was recognised as perhaps the major work on the rights of states and the duties of subjects), penned his original guidebook in Latin iambic pentameters, which may not have been the ideal vehicle for the task. Nevertheless, the 'Seven Wonders' provided a popular itinerary for visitors to the Peak, and encouraged an appreciation of the area's beauty and diversity. (The 'Seven Wonders', which still attract tourists, were: Chatsworth House; 'The Shivering Mountain' (Mam Tor); Eldon Hole; St. Ann's Well; The Ebbing and Flowing Well; Poole's Cavern; and Peak Cavern.)

During the 18th century, it was common practice amongst travellers in search of Britain's most striking landscapes to carry a 'Claude-glass': a mirror in an ornately decorated frame which was used to capture a scene in the manner of a painting by Claude Lorrain and other Romantic artists popular at the time. This curious 'aid' to enjoyment of the countryside may now be an object of ridicule, but before rushing to judgement with derisive hoots, consider the modern, able-bodied car-tourist who 'appreciates' the countryside through the windows of a steel box; he has, if anything, an even vaguer perception of the landscape than his glass-wielding forebears, who at least stretched their legs occasionally.

Although a taste for wilder scenery steadily grew amongst early tourists, walking on the high moors of the Dark Peak was almost unheard of until the late 19th century, when people from the growing industrial towns began to sow the seeds which were to lead to the establishment of Britain's first National Park. By the simple defiant act of 'trespass', working men and women challenged the feudal control of moorland owners and initiated a tradition of hard walking and climbing in the Peak; a development which was a world apart from the activities of the leisured enthusiasts who dominated climbing and rambling in Wales and the Lakes.

EARLY BOGTROTTERS

An important victory in the struggle for access to the moors of the Dark Peak came in 1897, when the long and extremely frustrating negotiations between the Peak District and Northern Counties Footpath Preservation Society and landowners finally reached a conclusion: the footpath running from Hayfield to the Snake Inn – the famous Snake Path – was, indeed, an ancient right-of-way. The route was restored to its former status, but not without a good deal of resistance from the local landowners.

The Snake Path was one of the many victims of the Enclosures, when traditional routes could be closed subject to certain conditions: prior to closure, notices were placed in prominent positions, to inform locals of the intention to remove rights of passage; this was, ostensibly, to allow would-be dissenters an opportunity to voice their objections. The notices were usually written in legal jargon which – then as now – tended to obfuscate rather than illuminate the rights of the common man. Should an unusually literate peasant or smallholder attempt to protest, he was then faced with the task of proving that the path had been regularly used for centuries. The Peak District and Northern Counties Footpath Preservation Society, funded by public donations, managed to prove that the Snake Path had been used from "time immemorial", and thus secured for future generations the right to cross the Kinder area.

Access to the plateau of Kinder Scout was a rather different matter. The moors were jealously guarded by gamekeepers, many of whom were more than prepared to hand out their own brand of summary 'justice'. The early bogtrotters responded to this challenge in different ways: avoiding the attentions of 'keepers was a sport in itself, for some; for others, the denial of the freedom to roam was a source of bitter frustration. There were ramblers who patiently applied for permits, and were sometimes allowed onto the moors for a day "by kind permission of the landowner". Others baulked at this 'forelock tugging' process and regularly ran the gauntlet by walking on moorland whenever they wished, regardless of the whims of landowners and their agents.

A major development in the history of walking and climbing in the Peak was the birth and growth of clubs formed by the few connoisseurs of forbidden moorland. These pioneering organisations held regular meets in the hills and quickly expanded their knowledge of the less-frequented parts of the Dark Peak; long-distance walks were established and many fine crags – not least of all, the magnificent gritstone edges – were explored. At the forefront of this remarkable period of discovery was J W Puttrell, a name synonymous with early gritstone climbing. James William Puttrell had begun bogtrotting whilst barely in his teens, and was a lone voice in the wilderness for some years. In 1900, with a growing number of converts to the cause of hard moorland walking and gritstone climbing, JWP and the newly-formed Kyndwr Club began to consolidate the achievements of earlier explorations on crags such as Wharncliffe, Stanage Edge, Froggatt and Curbar Edges, Nether Tor and the Kinder Downfall amphitheatre; the club, with members from Sheffield and Derby, opened up 'new' areas, including the Roaches and Hen Cloud in the Staffordshire gritstone area. This insatiable group, not content with surface forays, often turned its attention to the limestone caves and pot-holes of the Peak, and several hairy descents were made by Puttrell and friends during the early years of the century, particularly in the Castleton area.

Other clubs, including the Sheffield Clarion Ramblers (1900) and the Manchester Rucksack Club (1902), were founded, and important names in the history of the Peak National Park emerged: G.H.B. Ward of the Sheffield Clarion was to become a prime mover in the organised trespasses and rallies held in support of an Access to Mountains Bill, and was also a founder member of the Peak Branch of the Council for the Preservation of Rural England.

Less formal, loosely-knit groups began to grow, and gamekeepers during the early 1900s sometimes faced the prospect of attempting to eject men who held fierce convictions (and had the physical strength to back up those beliefs, if necessary) from the moors. It was during these formative years of walking and climbing in the Peak that the now classic Marsden-Edale bogtrot was developed by Cecil Dawson; 'The Colonel', to the hardy band of bogtrotters which grew around him (a group which included Alf Schaanning, Norwegian pioneer of Stanage Edge and one of the first to complete the challenging Derwent Watershed walk; and Louise Dutton, the first woman to walk the Pennine Way).

THE OUTDOOR MOVEMENT

Following the appalling carnage of the Great War, rambling and climbing grew in popularity and pressure for access to the moors and gritstone crags began to build as 'class consciousness' took root amongst the working populations of the industrial towns surrounding the Peak. The moors offered an escape from the poor living conditions which were the norm for many in the 'land fit for heroes', and whilst some ramblers were prepared to stick to the 'legitimate' footpaths, the lure of the high, open spaces provided an irresistible temptation to a new generation of people who, in common with a number of their predecessors and mentors, were unwilling to kowtow, even to those 'reasonable' landowners who were prepared to issue a small number of permits. The stated aim of the burgeoning Outdoor Movement was the acceptance of a right to roam over mountains and uncultivated land, and an end to the exclusion of the public from large areas of the countryside when no good management reason existed. As the number of 'trespassers' grew, so conflict between landowners – including the Water Corporations, who prevented ramblers from crossing publicly-owned land – and the access campaigners came to a head.

A fatal accident on Kinder Scout in 1922 strengthened the already entrenched positions of moorland owners, who could now argue that the denial of access was for the ramblers' own safety. Nevertheless, the post-Great War ramblers and climbers continued to inaugurate new walks over the barren moors and force new lines on the gritstone crags.

Later in 1922, Fred Heardman, Donald Berwick and H.E. Wild extended the Marsden-Edale to create the Three Inns walk (in particularly nasty weather); Heardman also made the first double Marsden-Edale walk and went on to play a vital role in the development of the Peak National Park from its inception in 1951, up to his death in 1973. As landlord of both the Nag's Head and the Church Hotel (now the Rambler Inn), Edale, he established the first Information Centre and Mountain Rescue Post, based at the Nag's Head.

With the coming of the Depression, huge numbers took to the hills in search of spiritual and physical revival; only to face being turned back by gamekeepers if they strayed from the few public paths. Access restrictions had been tightened in response to the growth of walking and climbing during the 'twenties, but the mass exodus of weekenders from the cities, travelling by train or bus, or even (particularly from Sheffield) on foot, brought new levels of conflict. Young people from the new sports and gym clubs, which had rapidly sprung up to channel the energies of frustrated, unemployed youth, increasingly turned to the great outdoors; and more than one bullying gamekeeper received a lesson in 'manners' from deceptively small and wiry wrestlers and weightlifters. Nevertheless, a code of conduct was developed; slowly, some farmers in the Peak began to adopt a benign attitude to the young enthusiasts from the city, and permission was granted – for a small fee – to individuals and small groups of 'regulars' who chose to make the most of their weekends by sleeping in barns. The owners of moorland, unfortunately, were more determined than ever in their resistance to the 'invasion' of the *hoi polloi*: in the mid-1920s rewards had been offered for the identification of 'trespassers'; in the early 'thirties the landowning classes clearly demonstrated that they were prepared to use every means at their disposal to prevent others from enjoying 'their' moors.

To publicly protest against access restrictions, ramblers and climbers held mass rallies in the Winnats Pass, with the stalwart G.H.B. Ward of the Sheffield Clarion Ramblers continuing the campaign for the freedom to roam thirty years on from the first explorations of the famous club. Yet, despite the popularity of the struggle and the on-going Parliamentary battles waged by sympathetic MPs, from Bryce to Mallalieu, the issue was given scant attention in the House of Commons. Given the lack of progress made by the official campaign for access by the National Council of the Ramblers' Federations, it now appeared to some that a rather more militant approach might be required if the stubborn landowners were to be effectively challenged.

THE KINDER TRESPASS

On Sunday 24th April, 1932, hundreds of ramblers outwitted police and gamekeepers to make a peaceful demonstration of protest by openly tramping over the hallowed grouse moors of Kinder Scout. In the aftermath, five of the ramblers received a total of seventeen months imprisonment: one man, John Anderson, was sentenced to six months for assaulting a 'keeper, despite the testimony of a police witness who agreed that Anderson was merely defending himself. Bernard Rothman, a twenty-year old unemployed motor mechanic and 'ringleader' of the mass trespass, was jailed for four months after trial by a jury which included three Colonels, two Brigadier Generals, two Captains and two Majors. Despite the judge's much vaunted 'apolitical' stance, the message was crystal clear: anyone who dared to challenge the establishment in the form of the landowning and grouse shooting interests could expect to feel the full weight of the law.

The first steps towards the fateful trespass on Kinder Scout were taken by Benny Rothman when he gave the Manchester Evening News an outline of his plans for an 'assault' on the heavily-keepered plateau. The subsequent report led to further interest, which was followed up by widespread leafleting. Hundreds of ramblers – estimates vary, from 400 to over 600 – met at Hayfield on the morning of the 24th April, as a result of the publicity campaign. Despite a heavy police presence, the ramblers made their way along William Clough in a well-disciplined manner, and progressed towards the rocky ramparts of Kinder Scout. Some 60 ramblers from Sheffield joined the main contingent, and although minor confrontations took place between ramblers and gamekeepers who attempted to block their way, the whole event was carried off with restraint.

After a meeting on the moor, the 'trespassers' dispersed; Rothman and a group of friends were amongst those who returned to Hayfield Station, where they were greeted by a welcoming committee of the Constabulary, and put under arrest.

The trespass, the arrests, the trial and the harsh sentences meted out by an 'impartial' judge; all gave a new impetus to the Access campaign, leading to a wider awareness of the need for the establishment of a freedom to roam. A national petition called for a review of the sentences given to Anderson, Clyne, Nassbaum, Rothman and Gillett at the Derby assizes. The Mass Trespass on Kinder Scout, hastily planned by the young working-class people who felt the most pressing need for access to the beckoning moors beyond the industrial cities, demonstrated the frustration felt by many people at the lack of progress made by the 'official' campaign – from which some working and unemployed men and women felt excluded – whilst the trial strengthened the view that it was rather naive to expect landowners to simply hand over access rights as a result of polite debate alone. Nevertheless, there were ramblers and climbers who were bitterly opposed to the Mass Trespass; the National Council of the Ramblers' Federations sought to distance themselves from Rothman and company, and it was suggested that the actions of these 'hotheads' had set back the Access Movement by fifty years. The debate continues today, and the issue remains highly relevant for future access disputes.

There are ramblers today who argue that Access Agreements owe as much to continuing acts of defiance by walkers and climbers as to the lengthy discussions between the National Park Authorities and landowners. Others suggest that 'trespassing' on forbidden moors and crags prejudices any further improvement in access. Individual conscience dictates our own response to present-day limits on the right to roam responsibly over the hills.

The 'riotous assembly' of the Kinder Trespass was not the first, and was by no means the last: the Abbey Brook Mass Trespass was initiated by the

Sheffield Ramblers' Federation in September 1932, to highlight the loss of land during the Enclosures, when enclosing landowners had effectively cut-off the ancient path over the moors, so that the right-of-way now ended at the parish boundary. The Winnats Pass Rally and the Cave Dale Rally drew thousands, and ensured that Access remained a burning issue. Individual acts of trespass continued, with numerous cases of conflict between ramblers and gamekeepers: the pressure for change could not be ignored; but it was not to come until after the Second World War.

CONSERVATION CAMPAIGNS

Many access campaigners became increasingly active in matters of conservation, largely through the Campaign for the Preservation of Rural England. In 1927, the CPRE, with the assistance of rambling clubs, had begun to raise funds for the purchase of part of the Longshaw Estate on behalf of the National Trust; the Trust secured the land in 1931, thus assuring that this area, at least, would be preserved for ramblers (no mean feat, given the poverty then prevalent). The CPRE went on to successfully resist threats to the Winnats Pass from road building plans in 1938 and, with Fred Heardman as a key spokesman, vehemently opposed the industrialisation of Edale. The Winnats Pass and Mam Tor (Thomas Hobbes' "Shivering Mountain") were acquired by the National Trust in 1943, again with the help of the CPRE, and a bequest from Edith Marples. But there were also defeats: after the Second World War, the fiercely-resisted development and extension of the Portland Cement Company went ahead and destroyed part of the Hope Valley; this gave us one of the most infamous eyesores in the Peak, namely the huge chimney which blots the landscape for miles around.

Concern for the environment grew with the rise of walking and climbing, and conservation and access have been closely linked for decades, despite the claims of those landowners who seek to totally exclude the public from the moors in the name of protecting the moorland wildlife and habitat.

POST-WAR DEVELOPMENT

Although many of the rambling and climbing clubs had fragmented during the War years, local activists were still finding new challenges: Phillip Brockbank, a leading light of the Rucksack Club, maintained the highest standards of hard bogtrotting, whilst cragsmen were discovering new routes and even new crags. Yellowslacks on Bleaklow was developed as a climbing ground by members of the Manchester University Mountaineering Club; and the Peak Climbing Club, founded as a successor to the Sheffield Climbing Club, continued the tradition of hard climbing on Stanage Edge.

The post-War Government was committed to a policy of full employment, and gradually the prospect of a trip to the Alps was to become a reality for some resourceful working-class climbers. The rise in education encouraged 'Outdoor Activities', and new guidebooks whetted the appetites of novices whilst challenging the 'expert' to fill the gaps; a time of opportunity hitherto unknown, with the British Mountaineering Council (founded in 1944) providing a new voice for climbers and hillwalkers, and the Ramblers' Association (the change of name from the National Council of Ramblers' Federations came in 1935) continuing to press for improvements in Access. But gamekeepers still patrolled the moors, severely limiting the enjoyment of anyone seeking the serenity of the high ground.

The report on National Parks given to the post-War Labour Government by Sir Arthur Hobhouse made it obvious that there was a desperate need for legislation which would allow access and protect the landscape from the demands of potentially destructive industry. The concept of National Parks owes a good deal to John Dower, whose own report in 1945 largely defined the structure and purpose of British National Parks, which are not owned by the nation; in contrast to American National Parks, such as Yosemite Valley. Much of the Peak's character is due to the fact that it is a living, working landscape, with established land use effectively maintained by residents.

The Hobhouse Report led to the National Parks and Access to the Countryside Act, 1949. Sadly, the Act reached the statute books in an emasculated form, with the principle of a freedom to roam (endorsed by Hobhouse) being replaced by Access Agreements to be negotiated between the new Park Authorities and the landowners.

The Peak became Britain's first National Park in 1951, but there were still regular disputes and conflicts (although few landowners went to the lengths of those who tried to 'deter' climbers by destroying the rocks: the owners of Windgather Rocks damaged 'their' crag with chisels; whilst the owners of Yellowslacks went further and attempted to blow up the crag with high-explosives). Despite such 'inconveniences', the post-War development of outdoor pursuits which had brought a major breakthrough in climbing standards continued, with the frontiers of possibility being regularly pushed back as a new group of working-class apprentices, spearheaded by the legendary Joe Brown and Don Whillans, honed their technique on Peak millstone grit. The best traditions of hard moorland walking were celebrated in 1952, when Phillip Brockbank and the Rucksack Club chose to mark the fiftieth anniversary of the group by linking the Cat and Fiddle Inn, near Buxton, with the Tan Hill Inn, North Yorkshire, in a walk of some 120 miles. The original idea to connect the (reputed) two highest Inns in England came from Fred Heardman, and the first attempt on this fierce moorland trek was made by Brockbank (who was forced to bail out, due to foot trouble), Neil Mather (who also had to retire, with a painful knee after completing 100 miles; he joined Brockbank on another attempt the following year, and on this occasion both finished the route), Ted Courtenay, Vin Desmond and Frank Williamson (who all arrived at the Cat and Fiddle Inn after walking for two days).

In 1956, part of the first and most famous 'official' Long Distance Path, the Pennine Way, was opened; although it was not until 1965 that the whole of the route was truly open to the public. The innovator of the Pennine Way was Tom Stephenson, who had penned an article in 1935 suggesting a 'Jubilee Trail' to commemorate King George's anniversary. The concept of a continuous route along 'the backbone of England' caught the imagination of many, and the Pennine Way Association was born: initially a route of 180 miles was planned, but this was extended in 1951.

The not-unexpected access wrangles continued, and some ramblers came to support the Pennine Way as a tactical move towards wider access, particularly to the Dark Peak moors traversed by the Way.

Although Tom Stephenson is most often remembered as the founder of the 270 mile Pennine Way, he was an all-round and indefatigable campaigner for the protection and extension of ramblers' rights in his role of first full-time Secretary of the Ramblers' Association.

The RA, the CPRE, the BMC, the Joint Committee for the Peak National Park, numerous Clubs and countless individuals, all played a part in the creation and establishment of the Peak National Park: although few of those directly involved in bringing Britain's first National Park into being were included on the Board, and thus, whilst the designation of the Peak as a National Park in 1951 was a just cause for widespread celebration amongst lovers of the countryside, voices of dissent were never totally absent.

The goal of climbers and ramblers – the freedom to roam responsibly over mountain, moorland, heath and other uncultivated open land – had not been achieved, and the effectiveness of Access Agreements remained to be seen; some campaigners questioned the ability of the new National Park Authorities to adequately represent ramblers and climbers in access disputes.

The first ever Access Agreement was negotiated by the Peak National Park in 1952, and the Broadlee Bank Tor Area together with 5,780 acres of Kinder Scout could now be freely enjoyed without fear of intimidation by gamekeepers. Other agreements followed and with more recent successes the Peak Park can claim to be leaders in Access. Nevertheless, power still resides with the landowners, who decide on what terms access will be allowed, or if it is to be allowed at all. Where access *is* granted, the landowners retain shooting or grazing rights and can claim substantial 'compensation' from public funds; the Park Authorities must also provide wardens and rangers to patrol the Access Areas.

During the early years of the Peak National Park, the wardening system – symbolised by officious red and green armbands – came in for a good measure of criticism, largely from those ramblers and climbers who were accustomed to reacting with two fingers to anyone even vaguely resembling a gamekeeper. Today, the Rangers are widely accepted as a part of the National Park and their broader role as conservationists and helpers of locals and visitors – a role which sometimes includes rescuing people (and sheep) in difficult and dangerous circumstances – has earned them more bouquets than brickbats.

It should be understood by visitors to the Dark Peak moors that Access Agreements allow for grouse shooting restrictions, whereby some areas are 'closed' to the public on the 'Glorious Twelfth' of August and on certain subsequent days during August, September and October. Notice boards are displayed at Access Points and information on the areas affected can be obtained from the numerous Information Centres strategically situated throughout the Peak National Park. Other exceptions to the rule in areas covered by open Access Agreements apply during extended hot and dry spells, when tinder-dry moorland may be closed to ramblers and climbers because of fire risk (meanwhile, drivers on the Trans-Pennine roads are free to stop for 'a smoke' by the road-side).

The Peak Park occasionally applies the 'Sandford Principle' – that is, where conservation and recreational interests are in irreconcilable conflict, the former must prevail – and the owners of grouse moors have consistently played the 'conservation card' whenever the 'threat' of public access has reared its head. The closure of the moors during rare hot weather has brought criticism from some members of the Country Landowners Association who have argued that the Peak Park Authorities have demonstrated "appalling irresponsibility" in their delay in closing the moors: "A plague on both your houses" might be the response from hard-pressed Access Officers of the Peak Park, at whom flak is directed from all directions.

Many ramblers accept limits on their right to enjoy the moors during hot weather; but those who oppose any restrictions on gritstone climbing and moorland walking emphasise the need for a freedom to roam: such a right of citizenship would not mean unqualified freedom to ignore the rights of landowners and farmers, but would lead to a break-down of polarisation between competing interest groups and would form a basis from which sound restrictions, for the protection of wildlife and the safeguarding of the legitimate rights of landowners, could be negotiated. Climbers have voluntarily refrained from practising their sport on certain cliffs during the nesting season, and moorland walkers almost invariably develop a wide appreciation of the fragile semi-wilderness which gives so much pleasure. Access Agreements have delivered much to walkers and climbers in the Peak National Park, but the freedom to roam responsibly has yet to be recognised as a valid use of land.

Outdoor enthusiasts must still resort to media campaigns, acts of protest (such as the organised mass trespasses held each year in September by the Ramblers' Association and others to mark 'Forbidden Britain Day'), and their presence in local enquiries if they are to continue to protect the countryside from powerful groups: the road lobby, which continually threatens to destroy forever some of Britain's most valuable landscapes, is able to directly influence policy-making levels of the Civil Service. Considering the constant menace facing our countryside from roads, forestry and other commercial development, the support of all who love and respect the land is vital if its fragmentation and destruction is to be halted. Such a lobby is unlikely to emerge if a majority are excluded from the places they are being exhorted to defend.

3

MOORLAND SAFETY

MANY of the suggested routes in this guide lie across high, rugged and often apparently featureless moorland, where rapidly-descending mist is an ever-present possibility. A reasonable level of fitness and stamina is assumed, as is the necessary competence in map interpretation and compass techniques. Although some of the walks – particularly those on the moorland fringes – may be completed without any real navigational difficulties arising, there are stretches of wild and pathless terrain which call for commitment and concentration. Be aware of the risks inherent in moorland walking and know how to deal with potential hazards before they arise. Don't wait until conditions deteriorate during a slog over Bleaklow before attempting to work out your precise location; monitor your progress constantly and always bear in mind the existence of possible escape routes which could offer a relatively quick and safe way off the moor. Watch for changes in the weather (which can be dramatic in the Dark Peak) and apply extreme caution when negotiating rocky cloughs after heavy rain or during a thaw following snowfall: attempting to ford a stream in spate is not recommended, and should be avoided by judicious route planning.

Walking on the gritstone plateaux of the Dark Peak can be particularly rewarding in the winter months, when a wet and sticky morass of peat, absolutely hell to cross for most of the year, may be frozen into something resembling solid ground and surprisingly rapid progress becomes possible; but, whilst a heavy frost or a light covering of snow provides some superb walking conditions, you will need to take into account the relative shortness of winter daylight hours when planning your route.

Beware of verglas-coated rock, especially when scrambling in the steeper cloughs: vibram soles can be lethal on ice. In heavy and drifting snow consider your route very carefully indeed. Floundering around in deep snow is an exhausting experience, and navigation is made all the more difficult by the obliteration of important landmarks.

So...why not stick to the low ground? The Dark Peak has many low-level walks which are extremely worthwhile, and the limestone dales offer superb walking without the worry of the consequences of becoming 'temporarily mislocated' (ie. lost). You are less likely to miss the bus (or the pub), and no-one is going to call you 'irresponsible': if you should fall and break a leg during a gentle riverside stroll, there is no need for an expensive helicopter airlift to carry you to safety, even in the depths of winter.

A walk in the dales can be an experience of unadulterated pleasure – which is more than can be said for a slog over Black Hill. So why not give the men and women of the Mountain Rescue Teams a deserved rest? It isn't the car-tourists who are seemingly unable to walk more than a few yards from their vehicles who need the services of the Mountain Rescue volunteers; it is the 'experienced' and 'well-equipped' walkers and climbers who have just run out of luck or made a miscalculation, usually in the most inhospitable regions of the Peak. Why put your own and others' lives at risk?

In fact, bogtrotters and climbers give serious consideration to their activities; they do not need protecting from themselves, despite comments to the contrary which regularly appear in the media. At the time of writing, the winter of 1993/94 has been marred by a number of deaths in the mountains of Scotland which has led to the Government and 'responsible' citizens questioning the rights of climbers and walkers everywhere to pursue their pastimes without insurance or certificates of competence. The possible introduction of an element of bureaucracy is anathema to most lovers of the great outdoors, whilst the petty-mindedness of those individuals who complain about the financial cost of rescues is beyond belief (presumably it would be advantageous to these 'taxpayers' if people were left to die on mountains). The introduction of compulsory insurance – against the cost of rescue – would regulate climbing and high-level walking: any form of registration and assessment ("are you experienced/well-equipped?") is bound to destroy the *raison d'etre* of the few activities where the players define the rules.

Whether climbing on Ben Nevis or walking over Kinder Scout, the individual assesses the risks. Adventure means danger, and an appreciation of rewards which run counter to the sad but widely-held philosophy of the old Yuppie T-shirt slogan: "He who dies with the most toys wins".

Perhaps the greatest danger of the Dark Peak moors lies in their accessibility and modest elevation. Kinder Scout and Bleaklow are 'safer' than the mountains of Scotland, but they should still be approached with respect: never underestimate the hills, whatever the prevailing weather conditions.

GEAR

Rambling is now part of the leisure industry. Full-page advertisements in the outdoor press, and even in national news-papers, extol the virtues of the latest in all-weather clothing and the breakthroughs in boot design. The (not inconsiderable) cost of promoting 'the best' is passed on to you, the consumer, who may well be completely bewildered by the array of 'essential' gear on offer.

Consider the early bogtrotters who walked for miles in their old clothes and often shivered through winter bivouacs – what would the insurance lobby have made of those decidedly ill-equipped adventurers? – not to mention the youngsters who started their climbing careers with a length of washing line and a remarkable faith in the granny knot. Whilst it would be irresponsible to advise inexperienced ramblers to wear standard Khaki Drill Shorts and a pair of plimsolls on the Dark Peak moors in winter, a reminder that expensive gear won't make you a mountaineer is certainly in order, given the rather grandiose claims of some manufacturers of outdoor clothing and equipment.

Quality gear won't ensure your safety, but it should definitely help. To begin with, stick to basics otherwise so much money may be invested in 'indispensable' gear that there is none left to fund trips into the hills. Whilst it is true that, as in some other facets of life, you get what you pay for, it is possible to equip yourself adequately without spending a fortune. Don't believe the hype. Think about the conditions you are likely to face and, to quote old BP of Mafeking, "Be Prepared".

Boots

Big Boots are no longer *de rigeur* for ramblers on low level routes: many wear trainers, which are comfortable and light, at the risk of wet feet;

wellingtons are adequate for short, gentle riverside strolls in bad weather; and, (far superior),lightweight walking boots with Vibram soles and uppers of suede and various man-made materials have become extremely popular. Nevertheless, for the crossing of moorland and attendant peat bogs sturdy leather boots with Vibram soles are undoubtedly the best, providing all-round protection for the oft-abused foot, and giving support to the ankle during an ascent or descent of steep ground – a vital consideration where rocky cloughs are involved.

An enjoyable day on the moors depends hugely on reliable and comfort-able boots, so choose carefully: try them on in the shop and ensure that they are 'broken-in' before venturing out on a serious walk. To give long service, boots need to be occasionally treated with waterproofing wax, paying par-ticular attention to seams and welts, whilst wet boots should be dried with care: more than one rambler has awoken after a pleasant overnight stay in a B&B to find that their kindly hosts have dried-out a sodden pair of boots in the oven – (don't do it). With modern padded walking boots one pair of loop-pile stockings should suffice, although some prefer one pair of stockings and one pair of socks worn together as a means of reducing undue friction (and adding warmth in winter, of course).

Bootlaces may be subject to excessive wear when crossing rough moorland, and a few marathon walkers sometimes carry a spare pair in their rucksacks. The risk of developing blisters can be reduced by the simple expediency of stopping to adjust your laces occasionally, although a concerted effort might be required to do this; once you have acquired a head of steam it is often difficult to pull up. (Some ramblers even spurn the idea of breaking for lunch, and prefer to eat on the hoof rather than interrupt a steady pace).

Further up the leg a little, gaiters are highly recommended in winter conditions and are useful for bogtrotting on all but the hottest of summer days. They are available in canvas, nylon and, more expensively, Gore-Tex and other 'breathable' materials.

Clothing

Long experience has established the importance of wearing layers of cloth-ing, which should give a degree of comfort as well as providing effective protection from the unpredictable elements. During just one day on the Dark Peak moors you may be battered by gale-force winds, heavy rain, biting sleet and driving snow, before being melted by glorious sunshine. Prepare for every contingency, and you won't have cause for panic when, (as they do), ominous, big black clouds begin to gather overhead.

For warm weather walking, shorts and T-shirts are ideal, but you will need to carry spare clothing: tracksuit bottoms, waterproof jacket and trousers, and a light sweater, at least. Temperatures tend to drop alarmingly and without warning on the moors.

A wind and water-resistant jacket is undoubtedly essential at any time of the year, but choosing the right type can be problematic due to the confusing array of fabrics and design features which may bewilder even the experienced outdoors enthusiast. Taste – or the lack of it – also plays a part, with the dreaded 'just do it' ethos reflected in active 'outdoor clothing' which has been designed with street-fashion, rather than genuine durability and performance, in mind. Of course, some of this 'urban groovy' gear might also be suitable for walking and climbing, but remember that many people care less about what they do than that they look right doing it; hence the large market for outdoor clothing (especially ski-wear) which is meant to be worn well away from the activities for which it *looks* like it was designed. So what do you *need*?

The wind-chill factor is a potential killer on the mountains and moors, and protection from wind and rain is absolutely vital. A serviceable waterproof and windproof jacket may be obtained quite cheaply, but you will have to pay more for 'breathability'. The increasing availability of breathable waterproof materials has all but consigned the traditional nylon jacket to the great rucksack in the sky; nevertheless, a relatively inexpensive nylon waterproof, which is lightweight and easily packed away, should perform the vital function of keeping the wind and rain at bay, although exertion may lead to an uncomfortable build up of sweat inside your clothing. The original breathable material – Gore-Tex – was developed by W. L. Gore and Associates in the late 1970s to deal with this problem specifically. Actually, no gear is *made* from Gore-Tex: the material is a plastic film which allows the free passage of vapour through billions of pores, whilst filtering out water. This laminate needs to be kept clean if it is to work effectively, which might possibly present a problem when crossing a black sea of oozing peat, particularly if you have opted for breathable gaiters.

After nylon was invented in 1935, and a way of making it waterproof (by slightly melting the surface of the closely woven fabric over hot rollers to produce a water-resistant glaze) was eventually found in 1948, the *cagoule* design emerged as the most practical for outdoor wear: relatively little stitching (which punctured the glaze) was required; the few openings meant few draughts or leaks; and it was extremely portable and light in weight. The only real problem was condensation, which remained the main bugbear even with the advent of two-way zips and pop-fasteners which allowed a measure of ventilation.

Gore-Tex tackled this perennial poser head-on, by attempting to balance heat and moisture exchange. Initially, numerous critics (who can't all have been exceptionally sweaty people) questioned the effectiveness and dura-bility of the new material, but today – after several modifications – breath-able fabrics are the first choice for many climbers and ramblers, if they can afford it; although Gore-Tex has now been joined by an army of fierce competitors, and prices vary wildly. Of course, there is no substitute for experience to know what you need, but you need decent gear to gain some experience, and even the expert cannot know how a new item is going to perform 'on the hill'. The outdoor magazines run regular gear reviews, which help, but they can only offer subjective impressions. Nevertheless, if you purchase a garment which is advertised as 'waterproof' – as opposed to 'showerproof' (an important distinction) – you should reasonably expect it to keep water out: if it doesn't, then take it back to the shop.

Traditional waxed cotton jackets, which were designed with the moor-land environment very much in mind, are another option: they are hard-wearing, windproof and, if regularly waxed, waterproof. Unfortunately, they tend to be rather heavy for more strenuous walking, and are totally unsuitable for stuffing into a rucksack. Condensation can also be a problem and, all in all, waxed jackets are less than ideal for bogtrotting, although they remain a reasonable choice for easier walking in inclement weather and are great for bird-watching, even if they are more regularly associated with the huntin' and shootin' brigade who generally prefer killing birds to simply looking at them. Waxed jackets usually come in muted green and brown colours, unlike many modern waterproofs which are quite often of retina-assaulting and aesthetically displeasing garish purples, pinks and the like: presumably, these shocking colour schemes make it easier for the Mountain Rescue Team to spot you; they might also be safer for those who stray – either by chance or design – beyond the Access Boundaries during the grouse-shooting season (depending on the temperament of the 'sportsman' holding the gun). An interesting and more recent development in waterproofing technology, based loosely on the traditional waxproof, offers portability and breathability in a lightweight jacket which can be reproofed with Nikwax. Further refinements are being made, and they cost less than microporous membrane and laminate clothing.

Waterproof overtrousers are available in breathable materials or (cheaper) nylon, and it is advisable to have a pair in your rucksack, even if you find you rarely wear them: on warm rainy days, some ramblers prefer to wear shorts and get their legs wet (which dry naturally).

Breeches are best for general bogtrotting conditions and modern designs utilising stretch materials have proven to be highly functional; they also shed light rain. More traditional tweed or moleskin breeches will keep you warm and should provide long service, but corduroy and heavy cotton tend to hold water, which could be disastrous unless you wear them beneath waterproof overtrousers during persistent rainfall. If you prefer trousers to breeches, then they should be tucked in socks and worn with gaiters on the boggiest ground or when crossing tangled heather moorland. Jeans are of little use in the hills, particularly in wet weather. (Almost every reasonably experienced rambler and climber is aware of this simple fact, yet who can honestly say they have never undergone the trial of having a pair of wet jeans clinging to their legs – then steam-dried, in the time-honoured manner, by standing dangerously close to the fire in the bar of a genuine country pub?)

Fibre-pile jackets have long been a favourite with outdoor types. Originally designed to go next to the skin with a waterproof over the top, fibre-pile is instantly warm and very light in weight. Unfortunately, the original fibre-pile jackets 'pilled' quickly – ie. small balls of material gathered on the outside of the garment – and gradually deteriorated to the point of virtual ineffectiveness as an item of warm clothing; this 'pilling' creates a shabby look, which seems to have been cultivated by certain individuals. Time was, – long before 'grunge' became a fashion commodity – when you didn't feel properly dressed in a climbers' and ramblers' bar unless your jacket gave you the approximate appearance of a moulting orang-utan (albeit a blue or red orang-utan). Today, fibre-pile has improved greatly with protective laminates to limit wear and tear. Ease of washing and the fabrics ability to dry out rapidly makes fibre-pile a practical choice, but if you decide to buy a jacket understand that the material works by trapping still air next to the skin: this requires constant contact which can only be achieved by a close rather than a loose fit.

Woollen sweaters can be acquired cheaply and are as effective and reliable as the most expensive outdoor gear, particularly if worn in layers. Two (or more) lightweight sweaters worn together trap warm air between them and, should the sun decide to put in an appearance, you can easily remove a layer.

Wool dries quite quickly and even wet woollen clothing will keep you reasonably warm. A wool shirt is therefore the most logical choice, and by undoing a few buttons you have instant ventilation. Breast pockets might prove to be useful. Cotton sweatshirts and T-shirts are practical and light, although a cotton shirt worn next to the skin will absorb sweat.

There is now a large demand for thermal underwear, from all-in-one thermolactyl combinations to cotton vests and long johns. A word of warning: underwear sold as "thermal" is not necessarily warmer than ordinary underwear. Damart appear to have cornered the market in warm, comfortable and breathable 'thermals', but there are plenty of cheaper alternatives available from high street stores. As always, you should avoid expensive 'elegant' stuff which reflects the style over performance priorities of the vacuous fashion industry.

According to 'experts', around one third of body heat escapes through the head: your own experience should demonstrate the indispensability of a hat in bad weather. There is plenty of room for individuality here: a flat cap – as worn by generations of hill farmers, who know more about sensible clothing than most; a grouse hat, designed for the moorland environment of the field sportsman and woman; or a wool hat, which can be pulled down over freezing ears and is unlikely to blow off, even in a gale (some types of wool hat can be readily converted into an extremely warm – but possibly itchy – balaclava); all will help to preserve vital heat. In summer, a lightweight (and light coloured) baseball cap or cricket hat will provide necessary shade from the sun.

Hands are extremely vulnerable under cold conditions, and gloves or mittens should be worn to prevent heat loss. In emergency, a spare pair of socks could be adapted (although this inevitably creates problems when handling map and compass). There are at least two other important reasons for carrying spare socks in your rucksack: if the pair you are wearing should wear out at the heel or toe they must be replaced immediately; and a change of socks at any time will give a wonderfully effective boost to flagging spirits – but especially when you have just washed your feet in a cold stream (and have taken care to dry them thoroughly).

A short scarf can act as an efficient 'draught excluder' in biting winds and snow flurries, whilst a lightweight cotton neckerchief provides a degree of protection for the back of the neck when walking under a blazing sun.

Other Essentials

A head torch – which is far more convenient than a hand-held torch – should be carried in your rucksack even where there is only the remotest possibility of being caught out after dark. A strong polythene 'bivvy bag' – available from most suppliers of outdoor equipment – could prove invaluable should you find yourself in the unenviable situation of having to sit out the night in open country. Carry basic first-aid materials on a long moorland walk: stretch-fabric sticking plasters are essential for the prevention of blisters; any cuts should be immediately treated with antiseptic cream; and a bandage and safety pins might be required in an emergency. In summer a high-factor sunblock may be necessary to prevent burning, whilst a small tube of lip-salve will protect lips from the drying and chapping effect of the wind in summer and winter.

Never neglect the 'inner man' when you're on the moors: try to eat a good breakfast before setting off. (Opinions inevitably vary as to which foods are best: a 'proper' breakfast to the author means a grease-fix of bacon and eggs, whilst many favour 'healthy lifestyle' muesli or bran and spurn the dread cholesterol.) Even if you are expecting to spend no more than a few hours on the moors, carry staple food and emergency rations.

A Night Out

If you are planning a 'backpacking' (an American word which has largely replaced the self-explanatory 'lightweight camping') trip, then you will obviously be toting a much heavier pack including a tent, sleeping bag, foam mat (e.g.,Karrimat: some novices forget this simple item, but brief experience will demonstrate the folly of doing so), stove and cooking utensils. Again, stick to basics. Weight is clearly a major consideration when carrying everything on your back from one overnight stop to the next, but don't sacrifice strength, warmth and comfort in an obsessive pursuit of the lightest possible load. Take a look around the reputable camping shops, pick up a few glossy leaflets and brochures and read the gear reviews and advertisements in the outdoor magazines. Remember the manufacturers are aiming to part you from your money; think about the conditions their equipment may have to withstand. Will that ultra-light tent stand up to a fierce moorland wind or torrential rain? Buy the best sleeping bag you can afford; a comfortable 'pit' is vital to morale. The Dark Peak is well provided with camp-sites and there are many opportunities for backpacking, but the nature of the terrain means you must pace yourself: over-ambition is a major cause of Mountain Rescue call-outs, so never bite off more than you can chew. Bogtrotting should be *fun*; tinged with masochism at times, granted, but never merely a brutal test of endurance.

Youth Hostels offer a worthwhile alternative for an extended stay in the hills, providing either a fixed-base, from which various day forays may be made, or an overnight stop on a long walk. Whilst you will have the advantage of a relatively light load on your back, bear in mind that hostels commit you to reaching them, whereas a backpacker always has the option of camping 'wild'. (For the more experienced, a bivouac – sleeping out without a tent – can be the simplest way of passing the night, but 'dossing' in open country cannot be responsibly recommended to the beginner, who should really gain practical knowledge of the hills through camping on 'official' camp-sites before camping 'wild' or sleeping out without a tent.)

Rucksacks

Most ramblers find that two rucksacks are necessary: a backpacking or climbing sack with a bivi-extension, padded back and shoulder straps, a wide hip belt which adds stability and support, and an internal frame; plus a smaller day sack. Cheap 'butty bags', which can be easily packed into your large rucksack if you are planning a series of days out from a fixed base (camp-site, hostel or B&B), are widely available, but if day trips from home are regularly made then it is well worth obtaining a sturdier day sack, which should repay the initial investment with years of reliable service.

When buying a larger rucksack, particularly if it has an 'anatomic' or 'ergonomic' internal frame, try it on and fasten the hip belt. The best backpacking and climbing sacks are expensive, so choose the right one for you. (Any reputable dealer should allow you to try out a 'loaded' sack for comfort and size.) Pack your sack so that the weight is evenly balanced and ensure that the items you may need in a hurry are near the top.

On the Dark Peak moors, carry your compass – and perhaps some emergency food reserves – in your pocket; the map should be in your hand or within easy reach at all times. A waterproof map-case (some people wear them slung around their neck – the effect is a bit 'trainspotter' rather than 'competent rambler') or a transparent plastic bag helps to prevent excessive wear and tear on your valuable maps.

MOORLAND NAVIGATION

For the walks in this book the Ordnance Survey Outdoor Leisure Map 'The Dark Peak' (1:25000) and a Silva compass are absolutely essential: don't leave home without them.

Moorland walking poses particular navigational problems: not least of all, the weather. It may be advisable for the totally inexperienced to turn back if the heavens look set to open or the mist begins to roll in, but if you back-off every time the weather worsens then it might take a lifetime to explore the Dark Peak; besides, there are times when the mist descends rapidly, cutting off your retreat or catching you out in the middle of a barren landscape, and you will need to know how to steer your way by compass if you are to reach your objective. Walking on a compass bearing, simple in theory, can be extremely tricky when you have a maze of peat groughs, hags and bogs to contend with. Experience in map and compass techniques should be gained on easier ground in good weather before you even consider crossing the high moorland plateaux, where confidence in your navigational ability may be somewhat stretched. But don't let this put you off; the subject of mountain and moorland navigation can appear quite confusing, at first, so be sure to keep the whole business in perspective. Rambling isn't a *technical* exercise intended to tax the brain: far from it. Competence in map interpretation and compass methods – which can only really be acquired through experience – will ultimately provide an open sesame to the wildest country and, before long, you should be able to handle almost any situation on the moors; confidently, and as part of a largely subconscious process.

Convenient landmarks: Holme Moss transmitter and the OS pillar on Black Hill summit

A full treatment of mountain and moorland navigation techniques is beyond the scope of this book and readers are respectfully advised to consult the bibliography (see Appendix), for recommended reading on the subject. The most important skill of all is map interpretation; avoiding accidents on the moors largely depends on your ability to correctly and quickly interpret landmarks on the ground and symbols on the map. Know your key conventional map signs, and make sure that the principle of contour lines is clearly understood, so that you can readily distinguish between the pattern of a ridge and a valley, and recognise steep or gentle slopes on a hillside at a glance.

The following brief notes are included for general guidance:

Setting the map

Given clear visibility, you can easily confirm your whereabouts by holding the map so that the major features on it coincide with the features on the ground. The map is now 'set'. This is a quick, simple and reassuring procedure, assuming there are identifiable landmarks and you know where you are in the first place. If the way ahead is less than obvious, set the map by compass: lay the compass flat on the map and rotate both map and compass together until the north indicator – the red needle – points to the top of the map. All perfectly straightforward, until the time comes when you find you are not where you are supposed to be and it becomes necessary to *calculate* your precise position.

Bearings and backbearings

If you are able to identify landmarks around you and are able to identify them on the map, you can pin-point your position by using backbearings, ie. by transferring the lines of bearings to the map. With a *Silva* compass the procedure is simple and accurate.

To take a bearing, point the 'direction of travel' arrow marked on the baseplate at the chosen landmark and turn the compass housing until the red needle is pointing to north on the housing. Now, correct the compass by *subtracting* the grid-magnetic variation (the value of which is given on the map).

To subtract the grid-magnetic variation, rotate the compass housing clockwise, thus reducing the angle at the index mark. This correction converts your magnetic bearing into a grid bearing. (Remember: whenever bearings are transferred from compass to map the grid-magnetic variation must be *subtracted*.)

Place the compass on the map with one edge of the baseplate touching the chosen landmark and move the *whole* compass until the housing north arrow points towards grid-north.

Draw (or imagine) a line along the baseplate edge and repeat the exercise choosing another landmark. The intersection of the lines gives you your position.

When travelling along a linear feature – you are following a ridge or a river, for example – then a bearing from one landmark should be sufficient to give you your position: your precise location will be where the edge of the baseplate – or a continuing line drawn from it – crosses the linear feature. Another bearing will, of course, confirm your location; always assuming you can identify a second landmark.

From A to B

So now you know where you are, how do you safely proceed? When crossing featureless moorland it will be necessary to take a bearing from the map and transfer it to the compass. This is an essential skill for bogtrotting and with a little practice taking a bearing should become almost second nature.

Place the compass on the map so that the baseplate edge joins up your present and intended positions (ie. with the arrow on the baseplate pointing in the direction you want to travel).

Rotate the compass housing until the housing north arrow points towards grid north. Now correct the compass by *adding* the grid-magnetic variation: rotate the housing anti-clockwise, thus increasing the angle at the index mark. This correction converts your grid bearing into a magnetic bearing. (Whenever bearings are transferred from map to compass the variation must be *added*.)

The *whole* compass should now be held level and rotated until the red needle is pointing to north on the housing. The arrow marked on the baseplate indicates your direction of travel.

Steering a straight course is rarely simple on the Dark Peak moors. Groughs often seem to be against your line of travel, and there may be barriers along your route which must be by-passed. If a detour is necessary, take a series of short bearings: focus on a landmark and head for it. When you reach it, take another bearing on another landmark along your route and head for that; by taking a number of shorter bearings you can steer a 'zig-zag' course past any major obstacle on your original straight line bearing, whilst focussing on a landmark ahead prevents you from straying off-course as you negotiate peat hags, pools and disorientating groughs.

Should you decide to retreat for any reason, turn the *whole* compass around (the direction of travel arrow on the baseplate will now be pointing to you), then rotate until the red needle points north; walk with the direction of travel arrow on the baseplate pointing towards you, until you have retraced your steps as far as your previous landmark, from where you may take a bearing in the normal way.

Timing

Allow yourself plenty of time to complete any walk on the Dark Peak moors, particularly if you are relying on public transport to get you home at the end of the day. Experience in planning and undertaking a variety of routes in the area is the only way to develop your judgement, so proceed judiciously and build on a solid foundation.

Naismith's Rule – the beloved formula of many fell-walkers – offers a flexible method of estimating how long your planned route should take: allow one hour for every three miles on the map, and add half an hour for every 1,000 feet of ascent. You may find that allowing one hour per 1,000 feet climbed gives a more accurate result, or that three miles per hour is over-ambitious; tailor the formula to your own personal requirements (according to age, fitness and experience) and allow for rest-stops, boot-sucking peat bogs and changing weather conditions. Remember that a quagmire in summer may be frozen into solidity (or at least, something approaching solidity) during the winter months: given severe ground frost, a moorland crossing may be completed surprisingly quickly – treat this as a rare bonus.

Assiduous timing and pacing between landmarks on the moors will serve you well should you be caught out by rapidly enclosing mist. If in doubt, it may be wise to retrace your steps if you feel that there is a strong possibility of missing your next objective – a triangulation pillar, for example – due to poor visibility: the consequences of passing a vital landmark could prove disastrous. When mist gathers and thickens, even hardened ramblers may experience a momentary flutter and the tyro should most certainly be forgiven a feeling of rising dread. Remember the big friendly letters on the cover of *The Hitchiker's Guide To The Galaxy*: DON'T PANIC! A clear head is essential, and concentration must be maintained against the eerie altered state produced by heavy mist. Trust your compass – you will have practised compass techniques in clear conditions on easier ground, and should already have acquired a certain amount of faith in its reliability. Walking in mist is never easy, but it need not be dangerous as long as you remain calm.

Never Walk Alone . . . ?

It is widely accepted that four is the safest number for a walking party: the general idea is that in the event of an accident one member may stay with the casualty whilst the two others go for help. Moreover, in mist your companions may be usefully employed as sighting marks: send one or two people ahead, near the limit of visibility and in line with the direction of travel arrow on your compass, and 'leap-frog' ie. walk up to your human landmark before sending him on again, until you reach a 'real' and recognisable landmark; this helps you to estimate distance and makes it much less likely for you to inadvertently stray off-course (which is quite easily done where groughs prevail).

Ideally, your initial explorations of the Dark Peak moors will be undertaken in the company of at least one experienced bog-trotter. There are also a variety of short courses, ranging from "Beginners' map and compass" to "Winter Navigation and Survival", held by the Youth Hostels Association; and Losehill Hall and other Outdoor Centres have regular navigation skills weekends (see Appendix). If, for any reason, these choices are impossible or undesirable, then you might enjoyably develop your abilities – gradually – in the company of like-minded, equally inexperienced companions, but remember that any party is only as strong as its weakest member; keep together, and if you venture onto wilder territory be sure you know (at least) the basics of navigation.

Should the beginner attempt a moorland crossing solo? The responsible answer is no; yet many top-class mountaineers began their adventurous careers with solitary forays on the bleak moors of the Dark Peak.

Solo walking can offer a tremendous feeling of freedom, but with the freedom to choose comes responsibility. In the past, accidents have been used as a lever to deny access; more often today, they are used in an attempt to compromise the cherished freedoms of ramblers and climbers by introducing control in the form of bureaucracy. When you are in the almost unique position of not being prevented from deciding for yourself what is or isn't an acceptable level of risk, don't abuse this rare opportunity through ill-considered action. It is always a good idea to leave word of your intended route (and to telephone at the first possible chance should you divert from your original plan); although some existentialist types may consider even this a form of compromise. The choice is yours alone; which is as it should be.

Route cards

Many ramblers and climbers have never filled in a route card (and probably never will). But route cards cannot be fairly considered as an imposition, for one very simple reason: they are not compulsory. Their main purpose is to facilitate any call for the Mountain Rescue services, but filling in a route card also helps to focus the mind when planning a walk. This could help to prevent less experienced ramblers from over-extending themselves; thus the chances of an accident are immediately reduced before even setting foot on the hill. Given the importance of route planning, the novice is advised to complete a route card before setting off on a moorland crossing if only because the procedure forces you to *think* before committing yourself: this discipline, acquired early, should stand you in good stead for the more ambitious projects you might choose to undertake at a later date. (If you leave a route card you must, of course, report any diversions, delays or your safe return as soon as possible.)

Grid references

Grid references are the most accurate way of pin-pointing a feature on a map, and six-figure references should be given when completing route cards (although the name of your starting point and destination – with named key points in-between – will often suffice).

Grid lines are the lines going horizontally and vertically across the map producing a network of squares. To give a grid reference, first take the vertical line to the left of the feature and note the number at the top or bottom of the map. Let us take Edale Cross, which stands at the summit of the old packhorse route between Hayfield and Edale, as an example. The number on the vertical grid line is 07. Now, estimate how many tenths of a grid square Edale Cross stands to the right (east) of this line to give the third number in the six-figure reference, ie. 8. The reference for Edale Cross begins: 078.

Next, note the number of the horizontal grid line immediately below the feature: in the case of Edale Cross, the number is 86, so the reference so far is 07886. To obtain the final figure, estimate how many tenths of a grid square Edale Cross stands above (north of) this line, ie. 1. The complete six-figure reference for Edale Cross is 078861. (For a *full* grid reference, the six-figure number should be preceded by the two letters of the relevant 100km square of the National Grid – these identification letters are given on the map: thus, SK 078861 is the full reference, although the letters are rarely necessary.)

SECTION B:

BOGTROTTING DELIGHTS

4

THE KINDER AREA

ALTHOUGH many refer to Kinder as the whole of the massif, Kinder Scout is the extensive, roughly triangular plateau of largely dissected peat bog which covers an area of some fourteen square miles. The highest point of the plateau – and of the Peak National Park – is marked on the map at Grid Reference 087876, and on the ground by a stake set in an old pile of stones. This point, at a height of 2088 feet/636 metres, is generally taken as the summit, but according to the Ordnance Survey there are actually two other 'summits' at Grid References 085875 and 084876, both standing at 2088 feet/636 metres. None of the three points seem noticeably higher than the surrounding landscape of peat wasteland, and the peak-bagger, intent on reaching the true 'top', may need to employ some assiduous compass work to locate the summit stake.

The Kinder plateau is notorious for its inhospitality, and in bad weather (which is hardly uncommon to the region) the peat hags and groughs might provide the uninitiated with a waking nightmare. Kinder Scout has often been compared with the battle-fields of Flanders; a reference not only to the suctorial terrain but also to the trench-like character of the deeper groughs – some of which have been viciously eroded to a depth of fifteen feet – intersecting the sometimes seemingly endless miles of peat. The First World War parallels can only be described as 'Over The Top': apart from the lack of gas, guns and barbed wire, there are no unbalanced Generals waiting to condemn deserters from this particular front; retreat from the plateau in appalling weather is a clear demonstration of common sense, not 'cowardice'.

In the very worst conditions, the Dark Peak moors can be extremely dangerous for the unwary or ill-equipped. Enveloping mists can descend at any time, and, in winter, a combination of freezing temperatures and limited daylight means that anyone attempting a crossing of moorland and attendant peat bogs must be constantly aware of his or her whereabouts and have sufficient knowledge of the area to be able to identify potential escape routes.

Nevertheless, it is often the hardest days in the hills that are remembered the best. Kinder Scout is a movable feast, and to truly know the plateau in its many and specific changes in mood this fascinating morass should be explored at different times of the year. There is something intangible about Kinder Scout. In winter, the eerie silence and strange isolation that snow brings to a place is intensified. Frost crumbles glutinous peat into lumps of coke and the brooks freeze into silence. The Kinder Downfall, undoubtedly the best known feature of Kinder, is at its spectacular best in conditions of prolonged air frost, when the river turns to ice on its tumbling descent from the Kinder plateau to the Hayfield Reservoir, and gargantuan icicles hang from the ledges of the rocky amphitheatre to form a glittering cascade in the sunlight of brief afternoon. Severe weather creates ideal conditions for ice-climbing on the Downfall, granting the enthusiast an all-too-rare opportunity to practise front-pointing techniques with crampons and axes.

At other times of the year the Kinder Downfall may be no more than a rather disappointing trickle, but there are occasions when it becomes a foaming torrent; given a south-westerly wind, the Downfall may be blown back – creating a striking sight and a good deal of spray.

Always excepting days of deep, drifting snow, the winter months often provide the best conditions for walking on the plateau. A penetrating frost solidifies the usually glutinous peat, and rapid progress may be made over sections which require iron resolve to negotiate in milder, wetter, weather. Against this, of course, must be weighed the sometimes Arctic temperatures and the short winter days. If you know the moors in summer, know them better in winter.

The Celtic *Cyndwr Scwd*, which referred to the Downfall, is the origin of the modern name although there have been numerous variants: *Chendre, Kynder, Kyndre* and *Chynder* have all been applied prior to the mid-eighteenth century. Any number of choice pejoratives have been used to describe the nature of the terrain, but Kinder Scout unquestionably holds a special place in the hearts and minds of many ramblers and climbers.

In September 1982, fifty years on from the famous act of public defiance when the Kinder Trespass entered the annals of working class history, the National Trust bought over 3,000 acres of Kinder moorland: an area which includes Kinder Scout itself and extends to their earlier acquisition at Edale Moor. The National Trust received grants of £315,000 from the National Heritage Memorial Fund and £75,000 from the Countryside Commission, and launched an appeal to raise an outstanding £200,000 from private donations. When the purchase was finally completed, ramblers and climbers could at long-last be assured that Kinder Scout would be protected and preserved for their delectation. But the development activities of the National Trust – including the building of car parks, visitors' centres and the blatant signposting in especially beautiful areas including Torriden and Glencoe – caused some concern amongst Kinder's many devotees. The Kinder Scout Advisory Committee was thus established – with Bernard Rothman, 'ringleader' of the Kinder Trespass as Secretary – to give representatives from interested bodies some outside control over the management of the area. The National Trust has, in the years following the purchase of Kinder Scout, committed large resources to the repair and restoration of this historically delicate region, and their efforts are widely appreciated.

Route 4(a):
Jacob's Ladder & The Woolpacks

Distance: 13 miles/21 km.

Start: The Old Nag's Head Inn, EDALE. (SK 124860)

EDALE may be reached by the Manchester-Sheffield railway line (opened in 1894) which runs through the Hope Valley. There are no regular buses serving Edale. A car park stands at the T-junction, near the railway station.

The Old Nag's Head Inn is the official starting – or finishing – point of the Pennine Way, and it has a long tradition as a 'ramblers' pub'. The original Peak Information Centre and Mountain Rescue Post was established here under the auspices of the late Fred Heardman (1896-1973), landlord – of both the Nag's Head and the Church Hotel – local councillor and legendary bogtrotter. The Peak Park's Warden Service (the first in Britain) was set up at a meeting held outside the Nag's Head Inn on Good Friday in 1954; the original limited role of the wardens was to patrol the new access areas. Today's Ranger Service has a much wider remit: indeed,should you arrive at a moorland Access Point during a rare heat-wave you may be turned away by a ranger, because of 'fire risk'. (Your response is, of course, a matter for personal conscience.) Moorland becomes tinder-dry during exceptional periods of prolonged hot weather; but bogtrotting and gritstone climbing are not known to be conflagratory pursuits. Whilst no-one should be in doubt as to the seriousness of moorland fires, any attempt by the Authorities to deny access is bound to cause controversy, given the past and continuing struggles for the 'freedom to roam' over uncultivated land.

Edale, which began as a group of shepherds' bothies or 'booths', is the name of the valley, and the hamlet commonly known as 'Edale' bears the name of Grindsbrook Booth. The road ends below the steep flanks of Kinder Scout, giving a feeling of the 'wild frontier': Grindsbrook Booth is a place which stands at the edge of things. Superbly situated and justly renowned as a major centre for walking and climbing, Edale has facilities for camping, an Information Centre and Mountain Rescue Post, a large hostel, B&B accommodation, cafes, a post office and shop, and two famous pubs: The Rambler Inn (previously The Church Hotel) and The Old Nag's Head Inn. The deserved popularity of the place can be a curse during Bank Holidays and summer weekends, and seekers of solitude are advised to find an alternative base at these times.

The following route provides an excellent introduction to the Kinder plateau, and the approach along the Vale of Edale, a delight at any time of the year, is particularly splendid in spring, when the greenery contrasts starkly with the brooding bulk of the deeply rifted Kinder Scout.

THE ROUTE

TO reach the Nag's Head from the railway station and car park, follow the road north past the Rambler Inn on your left and the Peak National Park Information Centre at Fieldhead to your right. The Information Centre is worth a visit, not least of all for the local weather report, whilst those so inclined may leave a route card here – Fieldhead is an important Mountain Rescue Post. (Next time you see a Mountain Rescue Services' collection box in a pub, make a donation; even the most experienced and well-equipped individual may come a cropper whilst out on the hill.) Continue past the Holy Trinity Church (1885) on your left and the original cemetery (dating back to the sixteenth century) on your right. The old stone and half-timbered, early seventeenth century Old Nag's Head Inn stands ahead.

To the left of the Inn is a stile, at the beginning of what used to be the 'Bad Weather Alternative' start to the Pennine Way, but is now the recommended 'Official' route. (Some wags have suggested that the only viable 'Bad Weather Alternative' start to the Pennine Way is to catch the train to Gargrave.) Leave the Nag's Head Inn behind and follow the Pennine Way, proceeding west below Broadlee Bank Tor.

In July 1937 a Handley Page Heyford (K6875) aircraft from 166 Squadron crashed into Broadlee Bank Tor, killing the six-man crew. The tragedy occurred as the 'plane was flying low and off-course; a story which was to become alarmingly common over the next few years, as aircraft flying in an area noted for high hills and low cloud increasingly came to grief. The RAF Mountain Rescue Units were literally forced into existence by the number of aircraft crashes in the hills. Today the Peak has a highly efficient Mountain Rescue Organisation, but by 1942 a small group of untrained

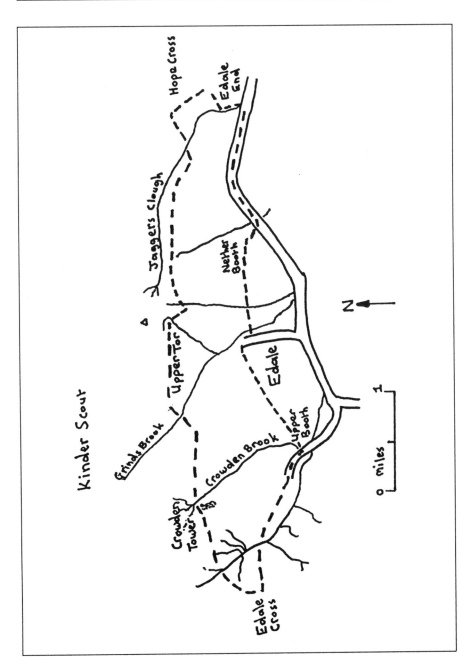

volunteers based at Harpur Hill, Buxton, coped with the frequent calls from police and farmers concerning crashed aircraft in the Peak. The men of 28 Maintenance Unit, Harpur Hill, attended some forty or so crash sites before becoming 'Official' in 1944. The RAF Mountain Rescue Service with its highly specialised equipment and training thus came into being. Nowadays, air crashes are fortunately fewer – but certainly not unknown – in the Dark Peak region, largely due to improved aviation equipment; today's Mountain Rescue Teams exist mainly to assist ramblers and climbers who find themselves in extremis.

Continuing below Broadlee Bank Tor, the path leads south-west to Upper Booth at the end of the Vale of Edale. A gentle walk through the farmyard and the Lee Estate (note the 'information shelter') brings you to the picturesque Yongate Bridge spanning the River Noe below Jacob's Ladder. This is a particularly fine example of a packhorse bridge, providing evidence of a former Jaggers' way. Often built on the site of a ford, these bridges prevented valuable loads from being swept away by a stream in spate; the low parapets lessened the risk of damage to the packs and their contents. Yongate Bridge remains as a monument to the Jaggers – or packmen – who regularly traversed the hills from Hayfield to Grindsbrook Booth and the villages beyond. Restoration work utilising the original stone has helped to strengthen the bridge.

This old packhorse route was known as 'Over Horse Waie', and is one of many ancient lines of communication crossing the country and surviving to the present day as living testimony to the ability of man to involve himself with the landscape.

You must now cross the packhorse bridge to reach the foot of Jacob's Ladder, where a girding of the loins is in order prior to the steep and winding ascent. Jacob's Ladder owes its name to one Jacob Marshall, erstwhile resident of Edale Head House – the ruins of which are nearby, at Grid Ref. 088860. Marshall cut steps into the hillside to provide a more direct (and much steeper) alternative to the packhorse way.

Maintain a steady pace as you climb this arduous hill, and watch your step for there is some potentially dangerous ground hereabouts; although some excellent erosion repair and maintenance work by the National Trust has helped to control the inevitable damage caused by the passage of countless boots. At the end of the Ladder a wide path continues west to the mediaeval Edale Cross (Grid Ref.078861), standing at the summit of the old packhorse way. This stone cross has been here for centuries but it has not always *stood* here: after being erected as a boundary marker by the Cistercians of Holywell (the shrine of Saint Winifred, patron saint of North Wales) Flintshire, who had been given land in the vicinity, the cross remained upright until time and the fierce Pennine winds conspired to render it horizontal. The cross lay where it had fallen, until 1810, when Thomas Gee of Ashes Farm, Hayfield, and his companions, arrived here with the noble intention of righting and securing the ancient monument. On completion of the task the men carved their initials and the year on the cross as a record of their achievement. (Latter-day vandals and would-be defacers should be warned that Edale Cross is now protected by law; the Ancient Monuments Acts were not in force when 'TG' and friends undertook their self-styled restoration work.)

Packhorse bridge below Jacob's Ladder (Paul Harrop)

Edale Cross (Paul Harrop)

From Edale Cross you may either retrace your steps east before turning left along the Pennine Way towards the hill known as Swine's Back, or head north from the cross via the obvious stile until you are level with Swine's Back; either way, your next objective is Edale Rocks. The Rocks provide an excellent landmark, as well as a superb coign of vantage.

Head North-east from Edale Rocks to Noe Stool – or The Anvil – above Edale Head and The Cloughs. The perimeter edges of Kinder Scout have many dramatic rock shapes and from Noe Stool, overlooking Jacob's Ladder, you now head east around the boggy Edale Head to the Pagoda, Pym Chair and one of the most fascinating collections of natural gritstone sculptures to be found in the Peak: The Woolpacks. Try to allow some time for exploring the Woolpacks: these weirdly eroded entities offer a unique experience. It is an especially strange place to be when low mist forms, hugging the ground like a mantle; eddying mist can create a mirage effect, lifting the vague shapes clear of the moor and adding to the surrealism of the images. Glimpsed through a thickening murk, the rocks loom squat and menacing; but these are friendly rocks,beacons and way-markers on the edge of the peat desert, offering shelter from the moorland winds.

> The Woolpacks and The Cloughs below have witnessed two aircraft accidents: in November 1945 a Light Transport Anson (NL 185) crashed whilst flying off-course in low cloud. It is believed that the pilot, who was killed in the crash, had set his compass incorrectly prior to take-off; in January 1952, a Harvard (FT 415) on a routine training flight crashed nearby; the wreckage and the body of the pilot were not discovered until five days after the crash when a group of ramblers came across the site. A few pieces of wreckage might still be found in the area (Grid Ref. 090868), whilst the Cheetah engine from the earlier Anson crash lies in one of the brooks (Grid Ref. 091866) which flow down the hillside to feed the infant River Noe. (Under no circumstances should wreckage be removed; it remains the property of the Ministry of Defence, and any unlawful interference with Crown property could lead to Civil or Criminal proceedings.)

From The Woolpacks continue east to Crowden Tower above Crowden Brook yet another magnificent viewpoint. Cross the brook and follow the path over Edale Moor, usually wet in places, to Grindslow Knoll (the slopes of which provide a skiers' play-ground, given the right snow and ice conditions). From the rocky top of Grindslow Knoll, above Fox Holes, follow the edge path around the head of Grindsbrook Clough and then bear north to cross the right-hand fork of the Grinds Brook. Double back along the east side of the rocky escarpments guarding the stream, and then continue along the path over Upper Tor.

On 31st July 1941 a Wellington Bomber (W5719), returning to base at Snaith after a bombing raid over Cologne was aborted due to heavy cloud and electrical storms, crashed into Kinder Scout. The pilot, Sergeant Parrott, had decided to return to Yorkshire with the full bomb load, but when the weather closed in as the crew reached the English coast it became impossible to establish their position; the radio had been disabled by storm and the Navigator, Sergeant Evelle, and the Wireless Operator, Sergeant Webber, faced a desperate situation: guesswork replaced technical navigation frighteningly often in the days before modern essential flying equipment.

On the night of 30th July, eight Wellington Bombers of 150 Squadron set off from Snaith: five completed the mission over Cologne and two others released their bomb loads over Belgium. The remaining Wellington, W5719, returned with its deadly cargo; only to smash into the Far Upper Tor area of Kinder Scout. The inevitable explosion blew the rear turret – and the rear gunner, Sergeant Earl Tilley – clear; Tilley, the only survivor, was eventually taken to hospital and a few months later was able to rejoin his squadron (he was later taken prisoner after being shot down over Holland).

...But back to the here and now: continue east over the crags, passing the triangulation pillar above Upper Tor. The gritstone cliffs of Upper and Nether Tor provide some high quality rock climbing for the competent, and their position overlooking Grindsbrook adds greatly to their attraction. Nether Tor still has some loose rock, however, and requires a rather cautious approach.

You now cross the lovely Golden Clough to reach Ringing Roger, the gritstone escarpment on the lip of the plateau; pause here for a while, and absorb the glorious scenery on offer. The Mam Tor – Lose Hill ridge (sometimes referred to as The Great Ridge or The Peakland Ridge) stretches before you, looking south, with the gentle Vale of Edale below. The ridge, separating Edale and Castleton, presents a perfect opportunity for an invigorating walk of around four miles, with several possible points of ascent and descent to and from the path which runs along the crest.

From the rocks of Ringing Roger continue to the rocks of Rowland Cote Moor on the eastern side of Ollerbrook Clough.

Near the head of Ollerbrook Clough and south-east of the Blackden Edge triangulation pillar at Grid Ref. 129878, another Wellington Bomber crashed during the Second World War. On the night of January 25th 1943, eight bombers from 427 Squadron dropped their loads on the U-Boat port of Lorient; unfortunately, the civilians of the French towns of Lorient and St. Naziare bore the brunt of the destruction, whilst the U-Boats lay in the safety of their concrete pens. Bomber Command did not yet have a bomb capable of destroying the pens, but it was hoped that damage to the Atlantic port's service facilities would provide a set-back to the deadly seacraft.

The returning Bombers landed at various airfields in England as their fuel ran low. Wellington X3348, flying in heavy cloud, crash-landed on Blackden Moor; miraculously, the crew survived without serious injury.

The crew of a Halifax Bomber, returning to base at Snaith a few months later, were not so fortunate: on October 5th 1943, Halifax HR727 of 51 Squadron crashed only yards from the Wellington site. Having completed an especially 'sticky' bombing run over Frankfurt, the four-engined Halifax was hit by fire from a Messerschmitt nightfighter and suffered damage to a fuel tank. Bad weather closed in as the radio failed, and the pilot, effectively flying blind, chose to descend below the disorientating cloud. The aircraft smashed into Blackden Moor: of the seven man crew, four were killed on impact and another crew member, Flight Engineer Sergeant Eric Lane, died later as a result of his injuries. Sergeant Lane was held largely responsible for the accident, after an inquiry by the RAF Flight Safety Organisation: rather a harsh judgement, (to put it mildly), given the specific circumstances of the crash and the generally dangerous conditions under which airmen were expected to carry out their duty.

...Returning to the route (but with one foot planted even deeper in the past): on the edge of Rowland Cote Moor stands the Druid's Stone, which provides yet another superb vantage point. The Druid link may not be apocryphal, and sceptics should note that not far away, to the east, on the barren Nether Moor, stands the site of an ancient Druid's Altar.

Head east from the Druid's Stone, crossing Upper Moor to reach Nether Moor. Watch your step as you traverse Upper Moor for evil peat pools lurk here, waiting to entrap the unwary traveller. Fortunately, a path from the Druid's Stone to the hill of Upper Moor offers a safe passage and you soon find yourself on the level ground of Nether Moor where a broken cairn on the eastern lip of the moor marks the ancient altar site.

Your next objective is Jaggers Clough. Descend from the plateau, making your way east over pathless heather moorland to the clear path below; an old gritstone wall runs past the quarry to guide you down for part of the way. Having attained the path, follow it into Jaggers Clough and cross the brook at the Access Point beyond the gate.

Continue easily along the path to the Crookstone 'junction', near Crookstone Barn – a Very Useful point of reference for ramblers on this side of Kinder Scout. Turn right (ie. south-east) at the 'crossroads' formed by the paths, and proceed along the course of the Roman Road, through a gate, to the ancient boundary marker of Hope Cross.

Hope Cross is inscribed with the date 1737, but it stands on a mediaeval site. The plinth on top, which directs you to Hope, Sheffield, Edale or Glossop, is a modern addition.

As you ascend gently from Hope Cross along the Roman Road towards Hope Brink – passing the site of an ancient chapel – stay with the straight, clear track until you reach the first possible opportunity to leave the splendid Roman promenade: this is provided by a footpath on your right which will deliver you to Edale End, standing on the Parish Boundary of Hope and Edale.

Pass through the small collection of farm buildings which constitutes Edale End and continue to Bagshaw Bridge where you go up the bank then through a gate, to emerge at the Hope-Edale road. Road walking is anathema to many ramblers (especially to those of the *genus* 'bogtrotter'), but the next brief section can actually be quite pleasant: turn right and follow the road in the direction of Edale as far as Nether Booth, which is to be found to your right. Now leave the road and follow the signposted path all the way to Edale (unless you are staying at the Youth Hostel, in which case you take the gate and entrance to Rowland Cote); passing through Ollerbrook Booth and continuing straight ahead for the Nag's Head Inn, or turning left after Ollerbrook Booth to emerge alongside Fieldhead and the Information Centre where, on reaching the road through Edale, you turn right for the Nag's Head or left for the Rambler Inn, Edale railway station, and the car park.

Route 4(b):
Kinder Summit & The Downfall

Distance: 11 miles/18 km

Start: The Old Nag's Head Inn, EDALE (SK 124860)

AT 2088 feet/636 metres, the summit of Kinder Scout is the highest point in the Peak National Park; but it is hardly the easiest place to find. The lack of notable landmarks could provide the inveterate peak-bagger with a nasty surprise.

The summit is no place to linger, and once you have arrived at the stake and cairn marking the (debatable) 'top' the suggested route demands further careful navigation to bring you safely to the highest waterfall in the Peak, the famous Kinder Downfall, before embarking on yet another crossing of the peat-laden plateau. A compass – and the ability to use it – is absolutely essential.

Some people are rather bemused by the fact that this bleak desert of peat supports a variety of natural life. Although the Kinder plateau is less noted for its wildlife than the vast Bleaklow, there is always a good chance of spotting mountain hares; particularly when they are wearing the white winter coats which contrast starkly against a background of rich, brown peat. The beautiful golden plover might be seen – or heard – as may other waders, and with luck you may glimpse a diminutive merlin, Britain's smallest bird of prey, or peregrines, which sometimes hunt over the Kinder plateau; you are virtually bound to see red grouse, flushed from cover by approaching boots. Kinder Scout certainly makes demands on ramblers, but the rewards are many and varied.

THE ROUTE

FROM the Nag's Head follow the original Pennine Way route which descends to the log bridge over Grindsbrook, from where an all-too-obvious path blazed by myriad boots leads on over the meadow and through a copse to the

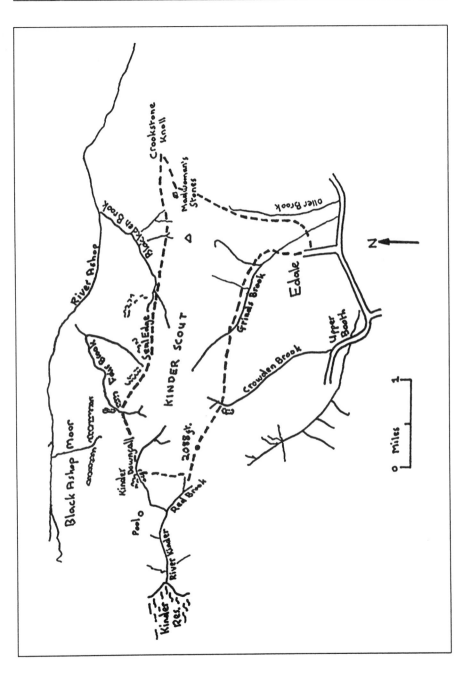

mouth of the deep rift which is Grindsbrook Clough. Stay with the clough, which steepens and narrows towards the top, until a fork is reached below the beckoning summit plateau. An easy scramble up the gritstone boulders of the left (North-western) tributary brings you to the plateau rim, with some outstanding views as a just reward following the uphill slog. 'Grinds' Brook is apposite: the trek up the rocky clough can indeed be a grind, particularly under inclement weather conditions. A word of caution: in freezing winter beware of ice-coated (verglas) rock, on which Vibram soled boots can prove lethal.

On emerging from the confines of the clough you enter a world of wide-open space and expansive sky. The Kinder plateau can amaze the uninitiated, and even the experienced rambler might be forgiven a tinge of apprehension on setting out across the peaty wastes, but for the present you stay with the plateau edge.

> Lying in a grough on Edale Moor at Grid Reference 101878 can be found two Cheetah engines and a few scattered fragments from an Avro-Anson which crashed here, 11th December 1944. The aircraft, with its contingent of Polish airmen, was en route from 16 Service Flying Training School, Newton, Nottinghamshire to Millom in Cumberland. Anson N9853 ran into dreadful weather over the Dark Peak; the pilot, Flight Lieutenant Chelstowski, dropped the Anson to a registered height of 2500 feet in order to check position. The aircraft hit the bumpy moor, ending up on its back. The crew survived the impact, but four of the six men on board suffered injury. Flight Lieutenant Mecinski, one of the two uninjured airmen, was able to make his way down to Edale to raise a rescue party. Four hours after the accident, the rescuers cut Flying Officer Klimczak free from the wreckage; he had broken both arms and a leg in the crash. The wireless operator, Flight Sergeant Pasinski, suffered injuries to his liver. All of the men survived the war, although Klimczak spent eleven days unconscious in the hospital at RAF Wilmslow. The altimeter of Anson N9853 had a 'permitted error' of 500 feet, a totally unacceptable margin for error when flying over the hilly and notoriously cloudy Peak. The investigating officers, however, chose to accuse the pilot, Cheltowski, of "gross carelessness".

From the rocky rim in the vicinity of Fox Holes, follow the path over Grindslow Knoll and continue west to the summit of Crowden Brook, which you cross. The rocks of Crowden Tower offer marvellous views over

Kinder Reservoir, from the western flanks of Kinder Scout (Graham Beech)

the verdant Vale of Edale; but a rather different prospect awaits. You must now turn to face the darkly brooding landscape of the Kinder plateau.

Take a compass bearing from Crowden Tower and summon up your powers of concentration as you head north-west over the peat hags and groughs towards the 'official' summit marked on the map at Grid Ref. 087876 as a height of 636 metres (2088 feet). If you are at all in doubt, and particularly if it is misty, it might be wise to defer this visit; the (alleged) highest point in the Peak National Park is actually a god-forsaken spot in a barren and bewildering landscape.

On reaching the summit cairn and pole, continue in a north-westerly direction to Red Brook (in summer the brook itself may not exist), where you join the Pennine Way on the western edge of Kinder Scout. Follow the Pennine Way over the summit of Red Brook, and head north along the plateau rim, enjoying the views over Kinder Reservoir to your left as you approach the natural gritstone amphitheatre of Kinder Downfall.

> At the Downfall, stop and savour the scene for a while, because another session of unremitting peat-bashing is in store. When you have rested and perhaps refuelled, it is now a case of "Once more unto the breach" – and should you stumble headlong into a peat bog you will resemble nothing so much as an extra from the battle scenes in Ken Branagh's film production of *Henry V* – so "Now set the teeth and stretch the nostril wide" for a careful journey over Kinder Scout.

From the Downfall, take a compass bearing on Fair Brook (north of east) and head out across the plateau. These moorland crossings are often a lonely experience but you might sometimes encounter the strangest people, particularly in the deepest groughs. Who hasn't met a lost squaddie – is it part of their training? – or heard disembodied singers, whistlers and hummers on the moors? The author once met a suitably dazed and confused Californian amidst the Kinder groughs; a greeting in the instantly recognisable West Coast drawl sparked a brief reminiscence about Yosemite Valley, before this traveller – who wore the best outdoor gear that a lot of money can buy and carried a juggernaut pack presumably stuffed full of the same – produced a motoring map of Great Britain (no compass) and asked the way to Mankinholes. (A brief reminder that the best gear isn't everything...)

On reaching the Fair Brook, at the point where the brook makes its descent from the plateau between Fairbrook Naze and Seal Edge on the north-eastern rim of Kinder Scout, make your way along the perimeter to the rocky Seal Edge and continue east to the Seal Stones – with some stimulating scenery to put the spring back in your step, should you be flagging a little at this stage. Stay with the edge of the plateau, and press on around the rim to Blackden Rind at the head of Blackden Clough which rifts Blackden Moor; and onwards, (ever onwards..) to Blackden Edge, from where you can enjoy views over the Woodlands Valley and Alport Dale.

(If you wish to curtail your journey due to inclement weather, tired muscles, blistered feet or an overwhelming desire for a pint at Edale, then you will no doubt be pleased to know that you are in the vicinity of the 'seven minute crossing': the shortest possible crossing of the plateau, north to south between Blackden Brook and the southern escarpment of Kinder Scout where you have a choice of descents to Edale.)

Continue along Blackden Edge and keep on heading a few degrees north of east, crossing the Hope-Edale parish boundary to attain the rocks of Crookstone Knoll; an excellent view point by any standards. From the Knoll, face roughly south-west and stride out, up and over a sea of heather and hardy grasses, to reach the collection of gritstone rocks known as the Madwoman's Stones. After the Stones, you commence a final fling over the bogs: south-west from the rocks is the head of Ollerbrook Clough, a few yards from the summit of Blackden Edge – the triangulation pillar marking the summit is visible from Madwoman's Stones; keep this in sight ahead and to your right, but you must also watch where you are putting your feet as you cross a minefield of peat pools and groughs to emerge onto the southern rim of Kinder Scout. At the head of Ollerbrook Clough, (south of the triangulation pillar and east of the gritstone escarpment of Ringing Roger) carefully descend alongside the Oller Brook to Ollerbrook Booth, where you turn right (ie. west) and follow the footpath to Grindsbrook Booth and the Nag's Head Inn (or right then left for the footpath which brings you to Fieldhead).

Route 4(c):
Black Ashop Edge

Distance: 7 miles/11 km

Start: The Snake Pass Inn (SK 113906)

THE A57 Snake Pass Road has acquired a national notoriety from its regular appearances at the head of the litany of snow-blocked routes delivered by weather announcers at the first sign of severe winter conditions. The name of this amphisbaenic road actually derives not from its convolutions but from the Snake Inn, which was built by the sixth Duke of Devonshire after Thomas Telford completed the famous turnpike in 1821. The Duke named his Inn after the serpent which forms the coat-of-arms of the Cavendish family. (Just to confuse the issue, the Inn is now called The Snake Pass Inn.)

(...For those who are wondering why the Duke of Devonshire should have so much influence in Derbyshire, there is a simple(?) explanation: in 1605, Sir William Cavendish was created the 1st Earl of Devonshire by King James I. When King James was told that the title to be bestowed was the 'Earl of Derbyshire', he replied that there was no such place as Derbyshire, and thus dubbed Sir William 'Earl of Devonshire'. The error was compounded in 1694, when the fourth Earl was created the first Duke.)

There are parking spaces along the A57 Snake Road, either side of the Inn; public transport is available from Sheffield, Manchester, Stockport and Glossop, but the services are restricted to Summer Sundays and Bank Holidays (check locally for details).

THE ROUTE

THERE is a small lay-by along the A57 Snake Road on the Ladybower Reservoir side of the Snake Inn at Grid Ref. 115903, on the north side of the road and about a quarter of a mile from the Inn. Across the road from the lay-by is a stile; Go through this and follow the footpath which descends

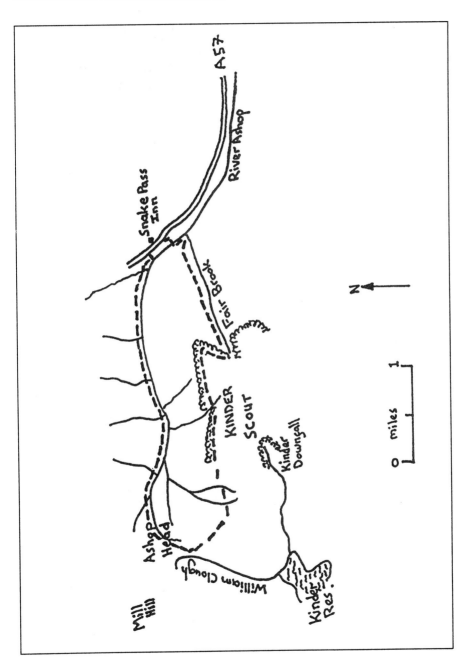

through the trees to a footbridge over the River Ashop. Cross the river and continue downstream to the Fair Brook. Ascend Fair Brook: ordinary care and circumspection will get you to the top without too much difficulty. The ground steepens towards the top, where you pass a small waterfall as you attain the plateau of Kinder Scout.

The major crags of the Fair Brook area are slow to dry after rain and are relatively neglected by climbers despite the fine routes on rough rock which reward a visit by the competent connoisseur: Chinese Wall and Fairbrook Buttress are the most popular, and there are many excellent buttresses along the length of Black Ashop Edge (simply 'The Edge' on OS maps, and often referred to as 'Kinder Edge').

Black Ashop Edge (Paul Harrop)

Having reached the rim of the Kinder plateau, there are now numerous opportunities for bogtrotting on a compass bearing: recommended is a lonely crossing of the peaty desert, with intermittent bilberry and crowberry (plants which appear to live on light and air alone), to the Kinder Downfall which is approximately a mile away; a return might then be made along Black Ashop Edge.

The present suggested route makes fewer demands on legs and navigational skills, with a well-defined path for much of the way. From Fair Brook,
turn right to Fairbrook Naze and then bear left (ie. west) to follow The Edge
overlooking Black Ashop Moor.

Continue along The Edge – which forms the north-western rim of Kinder
Scout – taking care on the more precipitous sections. This being a reasonably
straightforward walk, one which lends itself to a little dalliance, you might
take some time to examine the many oddly-eroded rock formations con-
tained within the two mile (3 km) escarpment. The Boxing Glove Stones
(Grid Ref. 078897), sculptured by nature alone, are a particularly famous
landmark.

Given clear weather conditions there are panoramic views to be enjoyed
along the whole length of The Edge: Ashop Clough runs below, with the
dreaded Featherbed Moss providing a barren background; beyond the
Snake Pass stands the Bleaklow massif, displaying its sweeping shoulders
on a dramatic skyline.

More than forty years ago, Black Ashop Moor was the scene of an aircraft
accident involving two Canadian 'planes. During the evening of the 22nd
June 1954, two ramblers spotted an aircraft wreck on the moor and quickly
notified the police. Search parties later discovered the wreckage of two
'planes and the bodies of the pilots; one of whom had a watch which had
stopped at 19.09 hours. The time of the crash?

Earlier that evening two Canadian Sabres – XD 707 and XD 730 – had flown
from their base at Linton-on-Ouse to take part in an exercise, and were
expected to return at 18.25 hours for refuelling. When the Sabres failed to
show, other bases were put on alert; but there was no sign of the missing
aircraft.

After the wreckage was found, only suppositions and theories could be
forwarded to account for the two Sabres crashing whilst flying fifty miles
off-course. There had been no radio contact or acknowledgement to base,
and the 'planes should have been out of fuel at 19.09 hours. The full
circumstances of the crash remain unexplained. Fragments of the scattered wreckage may still be found below Black Ashop Edge, but there are
no definite answers to the mystery of the Sabres.

At the western end of Black Ashop Edge continue west to join the Pennine Way on its obvious descent from the Kinder plateau, and follow the Long Distance Path as it crosses boggy ground *en route* to Mill Hill. At the lonesome signpost marking the 'crossroads' of the Pennine Way and the Snake Path (the half-way point of the ancient path from Hayfield to the Snake Road), aim for Ashop Head and be prepared for some heavy going, for this region at the head of the River Ashop is noted for its wet troughs of peat. Follow the Snake Path, which runs along the north bank of the River Ashop; high above to your right is Black Ashop Edge, a stirring sight which may go some way towards easing the mild torment of the initial sodden and sticky sections of this famous footpath.

Mercifully, the terrain improves as you weave your way east through Ashop Clough and, with luck, you may catch a glimpse of a ring ousel along the course of the river, or hear the highly distinctive piping whistle. Sadly there has been a marked decline in the population, largely due to habitat loss through extensive afforestation of upland areas, but they may still be spotted as they descend from the moors to forage for earthworms, insects and berries in the rocky cloughs and ravines, giving a flash of silvery wing feathers as they fly swiftly and purposefully through the deep gritstone valleys. Ring ousels are shy and tend to skulk under cover, but if seen the species is not difficult to identify: similar in size and appearance to the blackbird, the male has a diagnostic white band across the lower throat, whilst the female has a less distinct gorget and a browner, more subdued plumage; both have pale yellow bills. The birds arrive at their moorland breeding grounds by April, and begin their migration south to Africa and Southern Europe in late August or September and are gone by October.

Continue on your journey through the clough and enjoy the feeling of tranquillity contributed by the scenery of rock and water. After crossing Nether Gate Clough you soon reach the Boundary of Access Land and the coniferous trees of the Snake Plantation below the Saukin Ridge. The Snake Path leads you pleasantly onwards to the footbridge over the meandering brook of Lady Clough, which you cross before turning right towards the confluence of the brook and the River Ashop. The path now turns left, returning you to the Snake Road and the Snake Pass Inn where, licensing hours permitting, you might raise a glass to the Peak District and Northern Counties Footpaths Preservation Society who, after a long legal battle with local landowners, eventually won the right to walk on the Snake Path by establishing that this was, indeed, an ancient right of way; the path became 'public' in 1897.

Ashop Clough (Paul Harrop)

Route 4(d):
William Clough, Kinder Low & Brown Knoll

Distance: 11 miles/18 km

Start: The Visitor's Centre, Hayfield (SK 037869)

HAYFIELD is a popular base from which to explore the Kinder plateau and the western moors, being conveniently situated for Mancunian walkers and climbers. The village may be reached by train to New Mills station on the Sheffield-Manchester line through the Hope Valley and by bus to Hayfield on the Stockport-Hayfield-Glossop route. Hayfield and Edale may thus be linked by public transport, and numerous linear walks become possible even for those tied to a car. Parking is available in Hayfield next to the bus station and information centre, or at Bowden Quarry picnic area off the Kinder Road (Grid Ref. 048869). There is an excellent camp-site at Hayfield, which can be approached either by a short walk along the River Sett from the village or by the vehicle entrance opposite Bowden Quarry.

Hayfield, a rendezvous for the jaggers up until the late 18th century, grew with the Industrial Revolution; first came the textile mills, powered by the River Sett, then the print works – which once stood on the Hayfield camp-site – and the paper making factories, of which only one remains. With the development of the 'outdoor movement' of the Depression years and the post-War period, Hayfield became a major rambling centre. 'The Mountain View',a famous ramblers' 'caff' of this legendary era, once stood before Booth's Bridge along the Kinder Road, but only the foundations of the demolished building are to be seen today. Before the bungalow became a cafe, it was one of the several buildings in the valley used at the turn of the century by the 'navigators' employed by the Corporation of Stockport to work on the Kinder Reservoir.

North-west of Hayfield, and west of the small but delightful hamlet of Little Hayfield, stands the hill known as Lantern Pike, which is owned by the National Trust and preserved as a memorial to Edwin Royce, a campaigner for access to the moors and a past president of the Manchester Ramblers' Federation. East of the Pike is Park Hall, below Middle Moor, once the rather grand home of Joseph Hague, a 'local boy made good' who began as a pedlar before making his fortune – in the best Dick Whittington tradition – in London; having made his pile, he had enough good sense to return to Hayfield and enough money to move into the Park Hall mansion. A bust to Joseph Hague can be seen in Hayfield Church.

Hayfield has been hit more than once by fearsome floods which have claimed the lives of villagers. The present church (1818) replaced the earlier building which was swept away, along with several cottages and water-powered mills, as the rapidly flowing River Sett burst its banks. Even the dead have been disturbed by the floods; in 1748, when the raging river caused extensive damage to the graveyard.

During the mid-19th century the Kinder Downfall, swollen by exceptionally heavy rainfall, created similar havoc in the valley. Today, the Downfall in spate is a (surprisingly) rare, and extremely impressive, sight; particularly when a fierce south-westerly wind blows through the natural gritstone amphitheatre.

THE ROUTE

FROM the Information Centre at the start of the Sett Valley Trail by the car park and bus station, cross over the A624 (or under the A624 via the urban-style subway) road to Hayfield parish church and continue over the bridge; the route lies to the right, along the Kinder road, heading east towards the Kinder plateau. On reaching the Bowden Quarry – where cars may be parked – look for the commemorative plaque on the quarried gritstone wall, placed here on the fiftieth anniversary of the 1932 Kinder Trespass; a mass rally was held at the quarry, prior to the 'assault' on the flanks of Kinder Scout. (Campers with cars should approach the Hayfield camp-site by the entrance opposite the quarry.)

Press on along the Kinder Road, passing the detritus of the old Kinder Valley Mission (Grid Ref. 051873) and the 'navvies'' bungalow (Grid Ref. 052874): both sites are part of a rather meagre legacy from the period of the construction of the Kinder Reservoir; most of the buildings erected for the workers and their families have disappeared completely. The bungalow

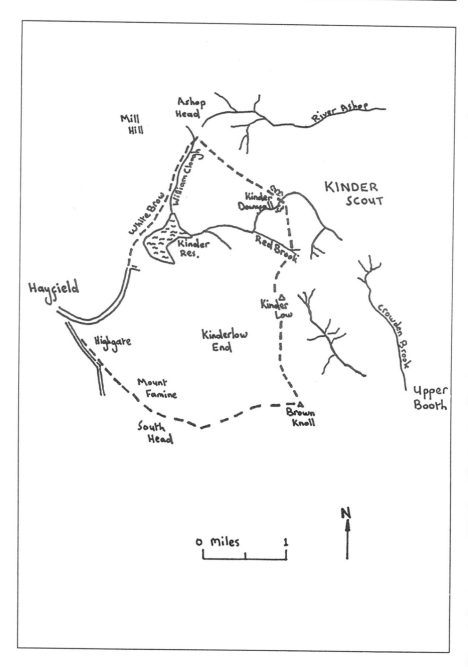

later became the famous 'Mountain View' cafe, a last opportunity for the Kinder-bound rambler's refreshment; today, only the foundations remain.

Descend along the Kinder Road to the point where it peters out, just before Booth. Cross the bridge and, ignoring the Farlands and Upper House turning, follow the footpath running alongside the River Sett. Cross the river by the footbridge; go through the gate beside the Kinder Reservoir entrance (No Access) and keep to the path up and on to White Brow. At the Boundary of Open Country Access Point on White Brow, bear right and continue via Nab Brow to the foot of William Clough, north of the reservoir.

(Kinder Reservoir has been the scene of some interesting water bird sightings, including shag, and the open oakwoods hereabouts hold woodpeckers and redstarts; birdwatchers may find a visit to the area surprisingly rewarding.)

The path up William Clough is well-worn and blindingly clear; proceed with due care and attention to the top of the clough at the path junction: left for Mill Hill, straight ahead for Ashop Head and, the present route, right for the Kinder plateau.

Attain the plateau by ascending the peaty path, and continue around the western perimeter of Kinder Scout to Sandy Heys; some shelter may be found amongst the rocks, but unless you are seriously flagging keep going to Kinder Downfall which is the traditional rest and refreshment spot, with views over Kinder Reservoir now far below. The Mermaid's Pool above the Reservoir is the subject of a local, long-standing legend: should you see a mermaid here on any Easter Sunday you will be granted immortality (and you are quite likely to be suffering from hallucinations brought on by serious exposure.)

Walk south from the Downfall, along the Pennine Way, to the top of Red Brook. As you admire the view from the summit of the rocky clough – the brook itself may not exist during prolonged dry spells – note the path which offers a pleasing descent to Hayfield (or a worthwhile ascent from Hayfield to the Kinder plateau) via the spur of Kinder Scout known as Kinderlow End.

The descent can be clearly seen as you cross Red Brook and, should you choose to return to Hayfield from this point, simply follow the path to Cluther Rocks (once the site of a quarry, as evidenced by the presence of

abandoned millstones) and on to The Three Knolls, which stand distinc-
tively above and to the east of Broad Clough. Pass over the curious lumps
to reach a gate at the bottom of Kinderlow End. Continue to the Boundary
of Open Country Access Point, which you cross to follow the footpath
traversing Harry Moor and carry on down along the path to Tunstead
Clough Farm. The footpath by-passes the farm buildings, to deliver you to
the ancient Bowden Bridge on the Kinder Road. Turn left and stroll along
the road, or follow the path through the camp-site along the River Sett, to
reach the centre of Hayfield village.

To continue the route from the summit of Red Clough, head south and
attain the triangulation pillar in the bleak setting of Kinder Low (not to be
confused with Kinderlow). The nearby 'mound' named on the map – and
marked by a cairn on the ground – is reputed to be an ancient burial site.
Bash on towards the landmark of Edale Rocks and then on again, south
along the Pennine Way route, passing the Swine's Back to meet the junction
with the old Jaggers' way: turn left for Jacob's Ladder and the Vale of Edale,
or right for Hope Cross and Hayfield (via the Stony Ford crossing and
Coldwell Clough). Our next objective, however, is the summit of Brown
Knoll; continue straight ahead (ie. south) up the hill, then south-east, and
cross the unpleasant, exceedingly boggy dyke to reach the triangulation
pillar (Grid Reference 084851) on the top of Brown Knoll. As usual, the pillar
is set in glutinous peat; but the views from the summit of Brown Knoll
should more than compensate for the squelchy morass underfoot. Imagine
the effect on the Edale Valley if the Sheffield steel company, Brown Bayley,
had succeeded in their concerted efforts to industrialise the area; thanks to
the resistance of the CPRE, ably represented by Fred Heardman and R.
Wright, the proposals were thwarted. (The Vale of Edale has also escaped
the creeping, soulless sub-urban development which curses certain areas of
the Peak where smart, modern houses stand where smart, modern houses
shouldn't. Not all of those posh detached homes were built before the Peak
National Park came into being, and it is difficult to escape the conclusion
that the Park planners must sometimes be facing the wrong way.)

On December 28th,1945, an Oxford (HN 594) aeroplane crashed into Brown
Knoll. The Oxford virtually disintegrated on impact, yet the three-man crew
miraculously survived. The flight should have been a short map reading
exercise carried out in a relatively comfortable heated cabin; battledress

was worn by the crew as heavy winter clothing was not considered neces-sary.

The instructor, Warrant Officer Robbie Robinson, was accompanied by two pilots who were undergoing 'acclimatisation'. The men – Flying Officers John Dowthwaite and Ted Croker – had acquired their skills in the azure skies of South Africa, and on their return to England were sent to the Advanced Flying Unit at Sleighford, near Stafford, to take a conversion course in flying multi-engined aircraft under British conditions; ie.in skies which are only rarely clear and blue.

Typically, cloud descended as the old Oxford approached the Pennines. At an estimated speed of 100 mph., the aircraft hit the top of Brown Knoll. The least injured of the crew was Ted Croker, who sustained injuries to both ankles. With only instinct to guide him, the lightly-clad Flying Officer crawled over the freezing moor through mud, mist and snow, and slid down the hillside where he discovered the old YHA which, at that time, stood next to Lee House. As he thawed-out by the fireside, Croker slipped into uncon-sciousness, but came round as he struggled to give the location of the crashed aircraft and his two companions to the Mountain Rescue volun-teers. A lengthy night-time search proved fruitless, and it was not until 10.30 am the following morning – approximately 20 hours after the crash – that the two airmen were found, wrapped in parachutes in a desperate attempt to keep out the biting cold. Due to frostbite and blood-loss, Robinson later had a leg amputated; Dowthwaite escaped with a badly-bro-ken leg. Ted Croker made a remarkable recovery: he went on to play football with Charlton Athletic FC, before becoming a major ambassador for 'the beautiful game ' as a highly respected and popular Secretary of the Football Association.

From the summit of Brown Knoll a descent may be made to Edale by following the path south-east towards Horsehill Tor, past the Boundary Stone. (Another aircraft crash occurred near here on 25th April, 1943: a Thunderbolt P47C 416227 of 63 Fighter Squadron USAAF crashed at Grid Ref. 093845, the pilot, 2nd Lieutenant John Coenen, having bailed-out barely in time.) Continue south-east to the Chapel Gate path: either descend along the Chapel Gate path (north-east) to Barber Booth or take the path (north) down to Dalehead and on to Upper Booth (or turn right after Dalehead for Barber Booth).

To return to Hayfield from Brown Knoll, head west then south-west along the Boundary of Access Land to the Access Point and the footpath running between South Head (to your left) and Mount Famine (to your right); stay with this path to the next Access Poin, then continue roughly north-west in the direction of Hayfield, via Chinley Moor Farm to the minor road. Either follow the road past Highgate Head into Hayfield, or, for the camp-site and Bowden Quarry, take the path on your right which brings you to the Kinder Road via Elle Bank wood and the footbridge over the River Sett.

Route 4(e):
Leygatehead Moor & The Snake Summit

Distance: 12 miles/19 km.

Start: Norfolk Square, Glossop (SK 033946)

STANDING just outside the Peak National Park boundary, Glossop is another excellent centre for walking in the Dark Peak and is particularly handy for the western reaches of Kinder and Bleaklow. Old Glossop, East of the town centre, remains as a part of the original village with several seventeenth century houses and a market cross. Glossop boomed in the 19th century with the development of 'Howardstown': the 11th Duke of Norfolk planned the new town on the turnpike crossroads and it quickly became a major centre for the flourishing cotton industry. 'Howardstown' swamped Glossop as the population dramatically increased, but the decline of the textile industries during the Depression years of the 20th century brought a marked slump to this little town with its numerous cotton mills.

To the north-west of Glossop, beyond the modern Gamesley Estate, is the 19-acre site of the Roman garrison fort *Ardotalia* or *Melandra*. A bad-weather walk along the flanks of Bleaklow via Doctor's Gate, following the course of the Roman Road (later, a mediaeval packhorse route) which linked Ardotalia to Navio, the central control fort at Brough in the Hope Valley, turns time inside out; you begin to understand why the Romans left Britain when the moorland winds and driving rain encourage craven retreat. (Not that occupying forces deserve any sympathy; but there was surely great relief amongst the Roman Infantry on being recalled to their sun-drenched Mediterranean homes.)

Glossop may be reached by bus from Manchester, Buxton and Stockport, and by rail to Glossop station on the Manchester-Hadfield line). The Glossop Tourist Information Centre at the Gatehouse, Victoria Street, offers advice on public transport, local points of interest and accommodation, should you choose to stay. Real ale drinkers might call at 'The Star' alehouse, Norfolk Street, which offers an inspiring choice of brews.

THE ROUTE

FROM the centre of Glossop, walk along the A624 road in the direction of Hayfield until (after a mile and a half or so of road walking) you reach the junction – on your left – of the A624 and the little road to Moorfield. Go down this road, (east), where you will soon reach a ladder stile and the Boundary of Access Land. Once you are over this, ascend to another stile giving access to the path crossing Shaw Moor. Follow the path (south-east) by the gritstone rocks known as the Worm Stones, and continue in the same direction over Chunel Moor to the Ordnance Survey Pillar at Grid Reference 045908. The pillar – 'Harry Hut' – comes into view (assuming there is no mist) at the top of the hill.

Head south-east from Harry Hut and stride out over pathless moorland until you attain the 'Grouse Inn – Mill Hill' path which runs roughly west to east over Leygatehead Moor (marked by poles and stakes). Pacing and timing is useful here: should you inadvertently cross over the path you will find yourself at Hollingworth Clough, with Burnt Hill (which lies south of Harry Hut) to your right (ie. west); in this event, retrace your steps until you meet the path.

The path over Leygatehead Moor is followed east to reach Mill Hill, which stands at a height of 1761 feet/544 metres. Before you reach the hill, look for the fragments of a USAAF Liberator Bomber which crashed at Grid Reference 058907; the remaining wreckage lies in a grough close to the path and to your left as you approach Mill Hill.

From the modest summit of Mill Hill (marked by a cairn and a stake – which is sometimes standing, sometimes not) you now head north-east along an infamous stretch of the Pennine Way, over Featherbed Moss – the word 'moss' might provide a warning – to the summit of the Snake Pass. It should, by now, be unnecessary to mention the necessity of using a compass on these bleak moors, even where there is a path. Mist can descend frighteningly quickly, totally destroying your sense of direction.

Your first objective from Mill Hill is Glead Hill; the path to Moss Castle and Glead Hill is marked by stakes and the summit of Glead Hill is itself capped by a thick post.

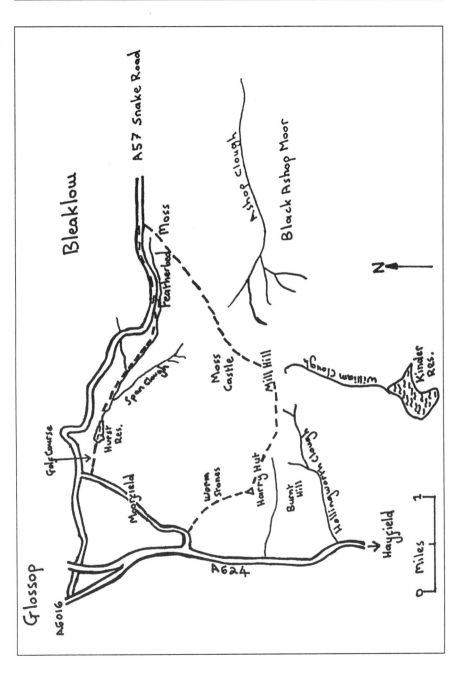

A USAAF Liberator, returning from a bombing mission, crashed at Mill Hill in 1945.
Wreckage lies in a peat grough near the Pennine Way (Chris Holmes)

Continue north-west over the dreadful bogs of Featherbed Moss. The
summit of the Snake Pass can be seen ahead – except in mist, of course – as
you trudge on. Your objective may be in sight, but it seems to take an
eternity to actually reach it. When you finally land on *terra firma* and find
yourself in the almost unique position – for a bogtrotter – of being delighted
to reach a busy road, decide whether you wish to stay on the Kinder side
of the road for the return journey; because a very worthwhile alternative
route to Glossop lies along Doctor's Gate on the flanks of Bleaklow (see end
of Route 5(b) – page 90).

After shaking temporarily free from the skirts of Kinder, purists and
Kinder loyalists should turn left – towards Glossop – at the point where the
Pennine Way crosses the Snake Road and walk alongside the A57 for
approximately one mile, around the bend to a point where Holden Clough
on your left (ie. on the south side of the Snake Road) may be attained. Carry
on down the rocky clough – in spite of a few snags, which are offset by the

always delightful impressions created by rock and tumbling water – passing Ramsley Clough which descends on your right, and continue beyond the confluence with the brook running through Span Clough (which divides Hurst Moor and Span Moor) to Hurst Reservoir. A gate provides access to the path which you follow around the reservoir and past the Glossop and District Golf Club House to Hurst Lane. Turn right for the Woodcock Road, or left and walk along Hurst Lane towards Moorfield until you see the footpath – on your right, before Hurst Villa; either way will deliver you easily to the relative fleshpot of Glossop.

5

BLEAKLOW

A suitable sub-title for any written description of Bleaklow might well be *'Fear and Loathing on the Pennine Way'*. Life is too short for some things: carp fishing, or reading *Finnegans Wake*, perhaps (would-be pedants please note there is no possessive case apostrophe in Finnegans Wake, the title itself being a Joycean pun); and, for some ramblers, the very idea of a walk over Bleaklow suggests not only excessive labour extended for scant reward but also an unacceptable level of discomfort; danger, even. Bleaklow, it could be said, has had a bad press.

The rather grim reputation of this expanse of moorland, peat bogs and groughs derives largely from the slanderous comments of certain Pennine Way survivors. The famous Long Distance Path traverses Bleaklow from the Snake Pass in the south to Longdendale, via Bleaklow Head, and for virtually the whole of this distance the path is a peaty mess; sometimes a hard slog, particularly when you are being persistently rained on and brutally battered by the tantrums of the wild, Pennine winds. For more than a few, this is the limit of their Bleaklow experience. The Bleaklow virgin would do well to approach this wholly unpretentious, deep-rutted and huge-shouldered hill with a mind free from malign preconceptions: perceptions are influenced by feelings, and the hills reflect our thoughts and affect our moods. Bleaklow is neither friend nor foe, neither sinister nor benign; just a hill, in fact. As you come to know Bleaklow, from gauzy morning to poignant twilight, having been pelted by rain and sleet, and dampened by dreary drizzle; having trudged through snow and wet peat, finishing your walk in the cold sepulchral darkness; or having started out on a bright, sunny morning in spring with the evocative sounds of the moorland birds carried on the breeze; then a touch of sentiment and familiarity may begin to creep in, and land once perceived as hostile territory is seen for what it is: a beautiful and extremely precious semi-wilderness.

Bleaklow can certainly be bleak, and it makes no compromise to slack navigation. Nevertheless, as long as you have adequate clothing to provide a cocoon against the worst of the moorland elements and your map and compass to guide you then you should be in command as you explore the Bleaklow massif. Never in *complete* safety – after all, the hills offer an escape from the irrational demands for certainty that restrict our lives so much. But, even with the unpredictable weather and occasional objective dangers inherent in moorland walking, you have regained an element of choice and control over your actions simply by setting foot on the hill.

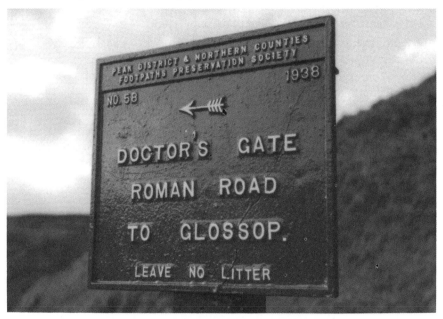

The sign at Doctor's Gate Culvert (Paul Harrop)

The dangers should be known and not overstated; but what cannot be exaggerated is the overall importance of the Dark Peak to the environment. Although grazing pressure and atmospheric pollution have caused heavy erosion, there are areas of Bleaklow where acid-resistant plants such as bilberry and cloudberry thrive amidst the heather and cotton grass. Bright green sphagnum moss colonises the badly-drained areas. Near the Barrow Stones above Ronksley Moor, the bushy Labrador Tea – a northern rarity –

has been found. Wading birds, including dunlin, redshank, snipe and golden plovers, may be seen and heard, as may the splendid curlew, with its haunting bubbling call. (Unfortunately for many species – including gargeney, whimbrel, golden plover, curlew and redshank – a recent agreement by European environment ministers means that thousands of birds, even those species protected in Britain, may now be legally shot by French hunters as they head for this country; the decision to allow hunting during the migratory season – Britain failed to object to the plan, as part of the Government's campaign to weaken European environmental laws in an attempt to lessen the influence of Brussels – was made in March 1994, and the effects on bird populations remain to be seen.)

Mountain hares frequent the high ground, as do weasels, and you may catch a glimpse of a fox. Common lizards are to be found in the more sheltered cloughs. One thing is certain: there is always much more to this barren 'desert' landscape than immediately meets the eye.

Route 5(a):
Wain Stones & Higher Shelf Stones

Distance: 10 miles / 16 km

Start: The Snake Pass Inn (SK 113906)

THE Bleaklow plateau may not be quite as high as Kinder Scout, and there are few of the steep-sided groughs which tend to disorientate the rambler when undertaking a Kinder crossing, but the vastness of Bleaklow and the shortage of obvious landmarks means that the hill must be approached with respect. Some individual rocks and groups of rocks are not named on the Dark Peak map, but those that are should be carefully noted; they have served as vital waymarkers for farmers, shepherds and gamekeepers – who usually named them in the first place – and now they provide ramblers with a means of finding their way over wild, open terrain, reinforcing the belief that the moors were created to walk on. The Wain Stones stand prominently before Bleaklow Head, appearing on the skyline as you approach the main Bleaklow ridge along the Pennine Way from the Snake Pass. Higher Shelf Stones and nearby James's Thorn are renowned vantage points (on a clear day) and are well worth exploring.

THE ROUTE

FROM the Snake Pass Inn walk north-west along the A57 Snake Road for a quarter of a mile or so, until you reach the footpath on your right which ascends the rather steep and thickly wooded slope below Dinas Sitch Tor. Continue along this path, beyond the tree line and on to the Access Point behind the Snake Pass Inn at the Boundary of Access Land. Do not allow yourself to be seduced by Doctor's Gate, which traverses the hill to cross Oyster Clough, for your route lies along the path running high on the hill – unmarked on the map but clear on the ground – with Oyster Clough below and to your right. Follow this path easily enough all the way into the head-waters of Oyster Clough. Walk north along the left fork of the clough

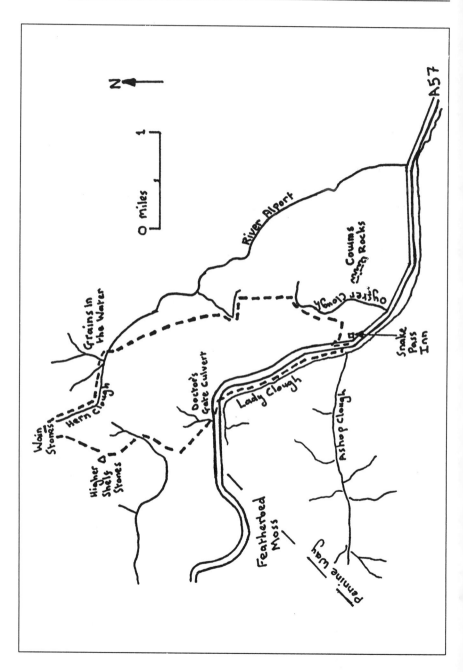

and cross this to face a pathless prospect which might intimidate the less-experienced; but with a little concentration this next section should provide few difficulties.

As you stand at the northernmost extremity of Oyster Clough, aim for your next objective – the channel from Nether Reddale Clough which lies almost horizontally on the moor (and the map) a little over half a mile north of Oyster Clough. Strict adherence to a bearing of north should keep you well clear of some nasty, wet and rather confusing terrain. On reaching the channel turn left (west) and continue into Nether Reddale Clough; there is now a sketchy path on the moorland perimeter leading to Upper Reddale Clough. Stay on this path on the rim of the moor (overlooking the River Alport to your right) until, about a quarter of a mile from Hern Clough, the path begins its gradual descent to Grains-in-the-Water.

From Grains-in-the-Water follow Hern Clough, west to the Pennine Way, then north along the right bank, until the end of the clough. You must now continue north along the Pennine Way, crossing a particularly soggy morass of peat to reach the Wain Stones, visible on the main Bleaklow ridge.

Dunlin may sometimes be seen in the vicinity of Hern Clough. These rather rare moorland waders – which are more likely to be seen in coastal areas in the winter – usually arrive on the moors in May, when they are in their summer plumage of chestnut and white with a black-patched belly, and begin to depart in July. Snipe is another moorland wader to be found on Bleaklow. This resident species and winter visitor is famous for the resonant aerial 'drumming' effect produced by the wind passing over the wing feathers as the bird performs its diving display flight. But perhaps the most evocative sound of the high moors is the bubbling spring and summer call of the curlew, the large, long-legged bird with its diagnostic down-curved bill; to hear and see these splendid buff and brown birds is one of the greatest – and usually unexpected – pleasures that moorland walking can provide.

Golden plovers are also more often heard than seen; their melancholy piping whistle is another of the plangent sounds associated with high moorland. The golden plover – should you be blessed with the good fortune to see one – is a beautiful bird, with a highly distinctive black and gold speckled plumage.

On attaining the group of weather-worn boulders known as the Wain Stones – the highest point of the route – head south to the Hern Stone then roughly south-west to Higher Shelf Stones, where you are rewarded with some magnificent views (weather permitting, of course). If you have the time and the inclination, you might scout around a few yards north-east of the triangulation pillar: this is probably the best-known of the Dark Peak aircraft crash sites, although little now remains of the Super Fortress which ploughed into the hill after the second World War.

Descend the grassy hillside south from Higher Shelf Stones then head south-east to Crooked Clough which you cross to reach an indistinct path which runs along the edge of the moor; follow this – with Crooked Clough below, to your right – and continue in a south-westerly direction; Crooked Clough loops away to the west and you soon reach the course of the old Roman Road along Doctor's Gate. Head south-east along the obvious path to the Doctor's Gate Culvert on the Snake Road. Turn left and walk along the Snake Road in the direction of the Snake Pass Inn until, near the bend in the road, you can leave the road in favour of the Forestry Concession footpath on your right which runs between Lady Clough on your right and the Snake Road on your left. Continue through the Snake Plantation to the River Ashop, where you bear left to emerge onto the Snake Road. Turn right at the road and walk the last few yards to the Snake Inn, where a rather different source of inspiration might be found.

Route 5(b):
Yellowslacks & Shelf Brook

Distance: 12 miles/19 km.

Start: Shepley Street, Old Glossop (SK 042947)

OLD Glossop is easily reached by walking from the centre of Glossop, although there is a bus route from Manchester (via Hadfield) which terminates at the top of Shepley Street, Old Glossop; there is also a local Glossop-Old Glossop service. As always when planning to use public transport in or to the Peak, check locally for details. Deregulation has worsened an already sparse bus network, particularly in the Dark Peak, and services have a tendency to change or even disappear without warning. The Peak Park bosses, who recognise that car drivers dilute the experience for others, are doing their level best to improve this situation (see Appendix), but it seems that unless you only venture out on Bank Holidays or Summer Sundays then some moorland areas will remain inaccessible without private transport.

Buses to Glossop run from Manchester, Buxton and Stockport, and trains on the Manchester-Hadfield line. Motorists may park in Glossop or along Shepley Street, Old Glossop.

THE ROUTE

OLD Glossop can be approached on foot from the centre of Glossop, along Hall Meadow Road to the church and the market cross. Shepley Street is beside the Queen's Arms, Old Glossop. Walk along Shepley Street past the old Union Carbide factory and the bus terminus, and stay on the track – part of Doctor's Gate – with Shelf Brook and Shire Hill to your right (south). Leave the track at the stile on your left which brings you to the Boundary of Open Country Access Point, and follow the path ascending Lightside ridge between Shittern Clough and Yellowslacks Brook, and bear right to

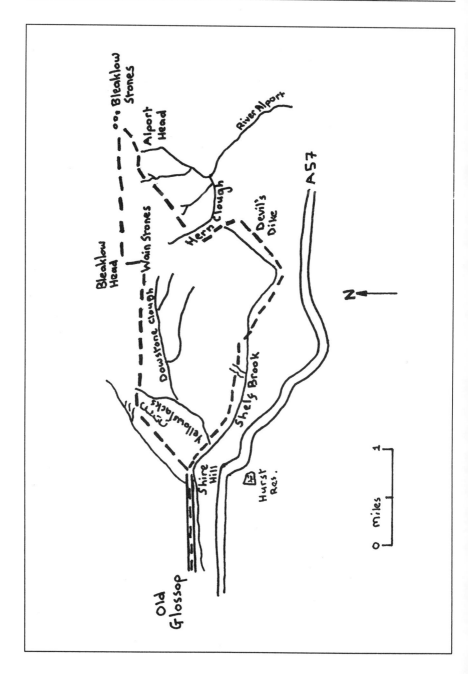

the top of the gritstone crags of Yellowslacks. Yellowslacks – previously known as 'Bleaklow Bastion' – stand in a fine position, high above Dowstone Clough; once a very popular crag with rock climbers (nowadays only moderately so), the owners of the rocks gave clear demonstrations of the strength of their feelings about allowing Access to climbers: in July 1963 and February 1964 the owners brought in contractors to demolish the crags with explosives; this desperate tactic caused some damage to the crags, but they still stand, fortunately – and rock climbers and ramblers now have free access to Yellowslacks. Sadly this is not the case throughout the Peak: attempts have been made by owners to charge climbers for access to some crags and a shocking number of MPs are suggesting that ramblers should be charged for access to specific scenic routes; there are still crags and stretches of moorland in Europe's most popular National Park which remain 'out of bounds' – "No Rock Climbing", boasts a blood-pressure raising sign beneath the delightful Bamford Edge; whilst moorland walkers still regularly face "Private" and "Keep Out" notices where there is no rational reason (such as preservation of privacy or land management) for such prohibitions.

Fortunately, this area is covered by Access Agreements; continue now, without let, hindrance, or pangs of conscience, across open land towards the top of the steep ravine of Dowstone Clough, east of Yellowslacks, and on to the Wain Stones which stand by the Pennine Way path. On reaching the Wain Stones, walk north for a short distance to the summit cairn of Bleaklow Head.

Bleaklow Head is the western point of the main Bleaklow Ridge. Prepare for some difficult going on this next section, across the Bleaklow ridge east to Bleaklow Stones, via Bleaklow Hill. A line of stakes guides you through the peat groughs to an area of open ground and the Bleaklow Stones, another rare landmark in this seemingly vast wilderness.

From the high ground of the Bleaklow Stones, head south-west and drop down the south side of the ridge where there is a path leading west to Alport Head. (Don't worry if you can't find this rather sketchy path; use your compass to locate the head-waters of the Alport, roughly south-west of Bleaklow Stones.) From the head of the River Alport, make for the head of Near Fork Grain; your direction is south-west over pathless terrain. On reaching the head-waters of Near Fork Grain you now aim west, towards the obvious bouldery rocks. From the 'Stones With No Name' (on the map, anyway – Bleaklow stalwarts call them the Fork Stones) make for the Pennine Way, crossing barren ground in a westerly direction to Hern Clough and the Long Distance Path; the Pennine Way over Bleaklow always offers a somewhat dubious form of sanctuary, given the wasted state of the path.

Freedom to roam? (Paul Harrop)

Having reached the Pennine Way, walk along it in the direction of the Snake Road, which lies to the south. Beyond Alport Low you will see the broad, shallow ditch known as the Devil's Dike which you accompany towards the junction of the Pennine Way and the ancient Doctor's Gate path at 'Old Woman'. Turn right (north-east) and follow the prominent path as it descends to Shelf Brook below. After crossing Birchen Orchard Clough you attain the right bank of Shelf Brook via the wooden footbridge and continue on Doctor's Gate, which gradually rises to the Mossy Lea Farm road; keep on ahead, staying with the ancient track which delivers you easily and pleasantly to Shepley Street and Old Glossop.

The Bleaklow massif is bounded to the north by Longdendale and dissected in the east by the wonderful gritstone valleys of the River Alport and the Upper Derwent. The dales have their own unique characters, and merit separate sections: thus, further suggestions for routes on Bleaklow are defined by their starting points and approaches, and appear under the relevant area heading.

6

ALPORT DALE

ALPORT Dale is dominated by the landmark of Alport Castles, a striking gritstone and shale landslip high on the eastern side of the River Alport. As with Mam Tor – Thomas Hobbes' famous 'Shivering Mountain' – the phenomenon is a wholly natural one: the spectacular result of soft shales worn away at the base of the escarpment below the hard millstone grit.

Explorations of the steep-sided valley of the River Alport should be planned with care. Although the gritstone gorge can be a delightful refuge in summer, in winter it can become a vicious wind-tunnel. Three Rover Scouts died of exhaustion and exposure hereabouts whilst attempting to complete the Four Inns Walk (extended from the Three Inns Walk – inaugurated in 1922 – to take in the ruins of the Isle Of Skye Inn, the Snake Inn, the Old Nag's Head and the Cat and Fiddle). This obviously challenging route, an annual Scout competition since 1957, was undertaken by the ill-fated party during March 1964. Sadly, the three young men were inadequately equipped for the expedition, and changes in the weather brought tragic consequences. This unfortunate incident is not related here to deter, but to serve as a reminder of the potential dangers (not that anyone should need reminding) facing walkers on the Dark Peak moors.

Alport Dale and environs provide a rare opportunity for watching peregrines, circling and soaring high above the moors on angular wings. Their spectacular power-diving 'stoop' to prey, hurtling downwards with wings closed, kills on impact as the impetus is transferred through deadly talons which grip the quarry in mid-air. These robust falcons, perfectly suited to hunting in open country, will also swoop upwards to take sometimes surprisingly large birds, and a merciless chase may ensue with hunter and hunted finally tumbling to the ground, bound together amidst the scattered feathers which leave the characteristic trail of a peregrine 'kill'.

Peregrines have made a remarkable come-back in the Peak: breeding birds were almost wiped-out in the supposed interests of the 'sporting shotgun' during the 19th century, and this unrelenting persecution continued during the 20th century as scarce nesting pairs were denied the opportunity to recover in the Peak by the concerted efforts of trigger-happy 'keepers. A national decline in the populations of some of our most magnificent birds in the 1950s, largely attributable to the DDT pesticide fiasco, was consolidated throughout the 1960s, and this serious reduction in numbers was clearly reflected throughout the Peak; it was not until the 1980s that an encouraging, positive pattern of breeding attempts by peregrines began to emerge. This time, a major threat to the survival of the Peak peregrines came from egg-thieves; but, with the help of the Peak Park Authority and the National Trust, known nesting-sites were protected by wardens in an attempt to combat the menace of the sad, anal-retentive types who – illegally as well as immorally – 'collect' wild birds' eggs or take young birds from the nest. Successful breeding and rearing of young followed, providing a nucleus from which an established population of Peak 'regulars' has slowly developed.

In recent years, peregrines have demonstrated a remarkable ability to adapt; in common with kestrels (which have utilised man-made nesting sites, such as old buildings and bridges, as well as colonising motorway verges), peregrines have been seen hunting in cities, where fat, urbanised starlings and the like provide an abundant, and ridiculously easy, prey. The cooling towers near the Meadowhall 'Leisure Shopping' (a contradiction in terms, surely?) complex, Sheffield, beside the M1 motorway, is one of several urban sites recently used as a winter roost by peregrines.

Kestrels are a familiar sight on the moorland fringes and the quieter sections of the gritstone edges, and are instantly recognisable by their characteristic hovering. A rarer sight is Britain's smallest raptor or diurnal bird of prey: the merlin, which may be found on the moors around Alport Dale and on the Kinder plateau. This resident breeder and winter visitor can sometimes be seen dashing fast and low over moorland in the Peak, twisting and turning as it approaches its quarry; which is often the ubiquitous – and in this instance unfortunate – meadow pipit. (In fairness to 'twitchers' seeking a 'tick', it should be noted that merlins are more frequently spotted on the southern moors, especially the Beeley Moor 'triangle' near Chatsworth.)

The sparrowhawk, which suffered a dramatic decline during the pesticide disaster of the '50s and '60s, is now a common resident species. Yet, despite the undoubted high numbers of birds in the area, they are surprisingly rarely seen as they roost quietly under the cover of dense woods and forests. The species has adapted well to upland afforestation, and the fringes of the plantations in the Alport, Woodlands and Upper Derwent Valleys might offer a fleeting glimpse of a sparrowhawk hunting in open country; and novice twitchers, in a tick-seeking triumph of hope over experience, might convince themselves that the female sparrowhawk they have just witnessed was a rare and elusive goshawk (but see *Derwentdale* section). Raptor watching is a rather specialised pursuit, but bogtrotters often reach the parts that many birdwatchers don't, and a basic knowledge of flight and general behaviour – 'the jizz', in birders' parlance – should provide yet another source of great pleasure and satisfaction for ramblers who are fortunate enough to see some of our most exciting birds in their natural habitat during a day out on the Dark Peak moors.

Walk 6(a):
Grains-in-the-water & Cowms Moor

Distance: 10 miles/16 km

Start: Alport Bridge (SK 142986)

THERE is most definitely an aura about Grains-in-the-Water. In freezing winter a profound silence grips this stunningly lonely place, and its transcendental lure can be dangerously seductive. Visitors should always be conscious of the shortness of winter daylight hours before extending their forays from this compulsive spot.

THE ROUTE

A stone stile on the left of Alport Bridge gives access to a footpath, which itself leads to the obvious track running from Hayridge Farm. On attaining this farm track turn right and continue to Alport Castles Farm, where you loop right to reach the footbridge spanning the River Alport. Cross the footbridge to the east bank of the river, but ignore the clear path which climbs to the top of Alport Castles: head north, instead, along the east bank of the River Alport and continue until you meet the first sizable stream. This is no gentle riverside stroll, and vegetation may impede your progress to some extent.

At the stream, ascend the hillside until a clearly defined path can be seen, about half-way up. This path runs along the hillside, crossing Glethering Clough and Miry Clough (a splendid waterfall near here repays further exploration), to deliver you to Grains-in-the-Water. Be prepared for some hard miles ahead.

From Grains-in-the-Water, head west along the north bank of Hern Clough until the stony stream veers north at the Pennine Way path. Follow the Pennine Way south-east, with a series of posts guiding your steps. At a double post, near Alport Low, the Long Distance Path goes south; from this

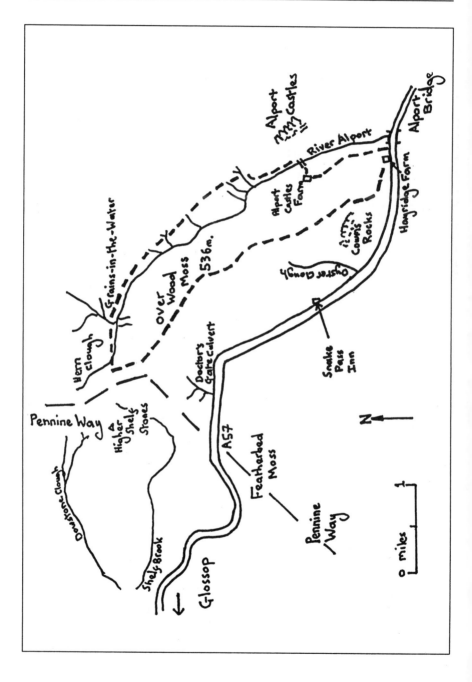

Alport Castles (Graham Beech)

point be ready to strike out over featureless moorland, leaving behind the relative security of the well-trodden Pennine Way.

Identify the height of 536 metres (1759 feet) on Over Wood Moss marked on the map and set off for it, on a bearing of approximately 120 degrees (south-south-east).

Having attained the high ground on Over Wood Moss, your route continues over the pathless moorland ridge which stretches for some two miles towards Cowms Rocks.

> A basic awareness of botanical protocol can be invaluable to the bogtrotter: beware the white, feathery heads of the cotton grass as it nods peacefully in the breeze, for this bulrush-related 'grass' denotes sodden terrain. Heather will not grow in the wettest ground, but this is meagre consolation when the tough and wiry stems, bushy at the base, become grasping talons which clutch at your boots and drain both strength and spirits as you forge ahead, not unlike Captain Ahab in pursuit of the elusive indefinable, over a varicoloured ocean. Fortunately, inspiration can be found to your left (ie. in the east); no great white whale, but the dramatic landslip of Alport Castles in full glorious view.

At Cowms Rocks, descend to the Doctor's Gate footpath along the old Roman Road and turn left; continue along this course, passing Hayridge Farm, then descend through the trees to the A57 Snake Road and Alport Bridge.

Route 6(b):
Grinah & Barrow Stones

Distance: 16 miles/26 km

Start: Alport Bridge (SK 142896)

GRINAH Stones provides a real view from the ridge. Facing south from the stones, the panorama administers a sensation of being right on the edge of it all – a truly breathtaking experience. The strangely-eroded Barrow Stones, which bear comparison with the splendid Woolpacks on Kinder Scout, offer a wholly natural exhibition of surreal gritstone sculptures which can be quite mind-bending when viewed through eddying mist.

THE ROUTE

AS for the previous route from Alport Bridge, following the path around Alport Castles Farm, attain the footbridge over the River Alport – east of the farm – and cross it to reach the foot of the path with ascends the hillside to the top of Alport Castles. Take this clear path to the top and then walk north-west above the landslip until you reach the point where the footpath turns sharply north-east to run between Fagney Clough and Ditch Clough and down through the forest to the banks of Howden Reservoir. Although this offers a delightful path to Derwentdale, and a clear escape route should one be considered necessary, you now spurn this easy and attractive option and continue along the edge of the moor, bearing north-west. Cross the forks of the stream and head for the triangulation pillar on Westend Moor, travelling west of north over some rather soggy terrain – the extent of which depends on the amount of recent, persistent rainfall in the locality.

On reaching the triangulation pillar, consider your next objective: The Ridge between the head-waters of the River Alport and the River Westend. The Ridge – named as such on the map – beckons you from roughly one and a half miles away to the north-west; but although the distance is short

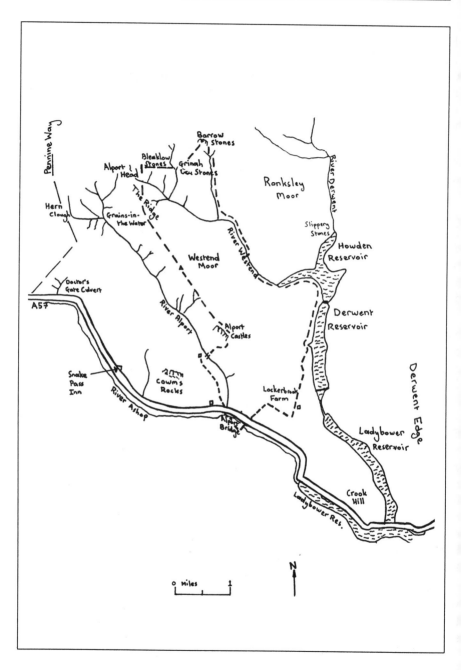

his is a region of wearisome peat pools and groughs, with paths which tend o perform wicked vanishing tricks – usually after they have lulled you into state of contemplation and dangerously false security. Astute bog-dodging and basic navigation – your direction is still north-west – will bring you o the rising ground leading up to The Ridge, where you make your way north to Westend Head.

From the head-waters of the River Westend ascend north, straight ahead o the main Bleaklow Ridge and the haven of Bleaklow Stones which stand at a height of 2060 feet/628 metres.

Next stop is Grinah Stones, one mile distant to the east, from where the views facing south are inspirational. Suitably invigorated, you now leave Grinah Stones for the third stage in this brief tour of Bleaklow landmarks: he large cluster of rocks known as the Barrow Stones, which is easily reached by a path which leads roughly north-east from Grinah to Barrow Stones. (Botanists may search for the bushy Labrador Tea which has been discovered growing in the vicinity.)

After spending a few delightful moments amongst the Barrow Stones, wrench yourself away from the main Bleaklow ridge and press on: south, down the hillside to the head of Grinah Grain. Descend Grinah Grain (with care) until you reach a less than obvious path – on the east side of Grinah Grain – which you follow down to the clear track. This old sportsman's path leads you easily alongside the River Westend and into the darkly beautiful – if alien – confines of the forest; cross the river via the footbridge before Black Clough, by the site of Blacklow Court, and amble along the track to the gate at the western extremity of Howden Reservoir. Before reaching the gate you will see a signpost on your right, indicating the clear path to the top of Alport Castles: a very worthwhile (and quite simple) approach to the landslip which could reasonably be taken now, although this means some retracing of steps – not an unpleasant prospect in this case – will be necessary from the top of Alport Castles to Alport Bridge via Alport Castles Farm and the Hayridge Farm track (ie. a reversal of the first part of this suggested route).

Alternatively, continue east very easily along the southern bank of the western 'arm' of Howden Reservoir by Hern Side, then bear right along the Derwent Valley reservoir road – Howden Dam is to your left. Continue south along the road beside Derwent Reservoir, with the Birchinlee Plantations on your right; the Birchinlee area was the site of the navvies' 'Tir Town', a remarkably self-sufficient community of reservoir workers and their families. Stay with the road, bearing right (east) by the western extremity of Derwent Reservoir and double-back on yourself after crossing Ouzelden Clough around the short 'arm' of Derwent Reservoir. (If the mini-bus service is operating – see *Derwentdale* – you might choose to give your feet a well-earned rest by travelling in comfort from West End down to Ouzelden; or, if you're enjoying the ride, to Fairholmes from where an easy ascent west can be made along a track to Lockerbrook Farm, to rejoin this suggested route).

Howden Reservoir, with frozen waves (Paul Harrop)

A short distance from Ouzelden Clough, along the road as you walk east, you will see a clear track on your right. Before launching yourself on this last leg of the route, pause at Wrenhey Coppice and soak up the splendid scenery of trees and water – a positively cheering sight, whatever the time of the year.

The track leads you from the reservoir road along the edge of the thick forest of the Gores Plantation to the buildings of Lockerbrook Farm (a track leads up from – or down to – Fairholmes at this point).

Continue on the track, leaving Lockerbrook Farm behind, until you reach a junction of paths: your route goes right, along the path towards Rowlee Farm via Bellhag Barn. (Another path also bears right, crossing the usually wet Rowlee Pasture to the top of Alport Castles; whilst other routes are available, straight ahead for Hagg Farm or left over Open Hagg to Crookhill Farm – below the distinctive Crook Hill – and on to the Ashopton Viaduct and the A57 over Ladybower Reservoir.)

Follow the track until you emerge onto the A57 Snake Road which you cross to Rowlee Bridge, spanning the River Ashop. Go over the bridge to the Boundary of Open Country at the Access Point and follow the path west to the next Access Point where you attain the course of the Roman road; this delivers you to a footbridge, by which you re-cross the River Ashop to the A57 Snake Road and Alport Bridge; your starting point and the end of the walk.

Rowlee Pasture – an alternative ascent to Alport Castles – was the scene of an aircraft crash on April 12th, 1941, involving a Defiant nightfighter on night flying practice and air tests. The two-man crew from 96 Squadron – Flying Officer Paul Rabone, a fighter pilot from New Zealand, and Flying Officer John Ritchie, from Scotland – abandoned Defiant N1766 when the radio failed during the flight through a black, cloudy night over the dangerous high ground of the Peak. Unhappy with the engine, the two men safely baled-out and the Defiant crashed into the hill at Grid Reference 154905. (John Ritchie roused the worst fears of a local farmer, who initially took the Flying Officer for an enemy airman – in Celtic tones, Ritchie finally convinced his would-be captor that he was, indeed, a 'British' Officer.)

A remarkable Official Recovery operation was undertaken in August 1980, when the Merlin engine of Defiant N 1766 was pulled from the mud of Rowlee Pasture – no easy task – by a particularly dedicated group of aviation archaeologists. The exercise was, of course, carried out with the full permission of the relevant authorities: Official member groups of the British Aviation Archaeological Society recover wreckage as part of a co-ordinated research effort, and do not simply steal bits of aircraft; unlike the unauthorised 'souvenir hunters' (a rather strange bunch, but the genus certainly exists) who hamper the work of recovery groups. (It is a criminal offence to remove wreckage from, or to be seen digging at, any crash site.)

The final stages of the previous walk should have whetted your appetite for the Upper Derwent Valley and the following suggested routes offer an opportunity to experience an area which is, for many visitors, the most spectacular in the whole of the Peak National Park. Derwentdale has something for everyone, whether casual day-trippers or determined bogtrotters.

7

DERWENTDALE

ACCORDING to the doctrine of Thomas Aquinas, those things are beautiful the apprehension of which pleases: Derwentdale, with its feast of visual delights, undoubtedly fits this particular, tolerant, frame. Yet the picture-postcard perfection of the scenery, calling to mind the almost stereotype panoramas of Scandinavia, renders this area of the Dark Peak an alien landscape where the hand of man can be clearly perceived. Nature surely supplied the basics but human agency has transformed the gritstone valley of the Upper Derwent, creating a spectacular vision which draws hordes of visitors throughout the year. But to suggest that the valley has been improved and the natural scenery enhanced by man is to recall the era of Repton and 'Capability' Brown, when it was widely held that nature needed some judicious assistance if a beautiful ideal was to be achieved. Nevertheless, careful management of the area – with an emphasis on conservation and landscape – has provided us with a veritable jewel in an oasis. A touch contrived, for some tastes, but no-one can deny the physical beauty of Derwentdale.

Respect for the Peak landscape and ecology was unlikely to have figured prominently in the minds of the water engineers as they conducted their search for sites suitable for damming and flooding. The Upper Derwent was decidedly exploitable, and a plan was formulated for the construction of six reservoirs, a number which was later reduced to three; the triple expanse of Howden, Derwent and Ladybower. The growing demand from expanding industrial cities for drinking water had led to the formation of the Derwent Valley Water Board – made up of the Sheffield, Nottingham, Derby and Leicester Water Corporations – in 1899, and work began on the Howden Reservoir in 1901, reaching completion in 1912. The Derwent Reservoir was built between 1902 and 1916, with several scattered hill farms being sacrificed to the rising waters of the great artificial lakes. The final, almost apocalyptic, stage of this Herculean feat of civil engineering came with the creation of the largest of the reservoirs, the Ladybower, between 1935 and 1943. The picturesque gritstone villages of Ashopton and Derwent were drowned as the valley was flooded, the erstwhile residents having been rehoused at Yorkshire Bridge below the magnificent 416 yards long earthwork embankment of Ladybower Reservoir, despite desperate attempts by the villagers to save their homes from the deluge. Along with the cottages, some historic buildings were lost to the demolition men in 1943: the parish church of St. John and St.James (except for the spire and tower, which occasionally made eerie reappearances until after the drought of 1959, when the Board had it destroyed as an unsafe temptation to the curious visitor); and the 17th century manor house built by the Balguy family, Derwent Hall, home to the Duke of Norfolk and later a Youth Hostel. Derwent Hall was purchased by the Derwent Valley Water Board and, before it was flattened, completely stripped by them – oak stairs, floors and panelling were flogged off to Derby Corporation at half-a-crown a square foot, and some was used to decorate the Board's offices. The original Packhorse Bridge at Derwent was saved, taken down and later re-erected further up the dale; the Water Board kindly shelled out the positively underwhelming sum of fifty pounds towards the estimated £1000 required for the project (the money was raised by public subscription and the bridge now stands at Slippery Stones, north of Howden Reservoir, with a dedication to Sheffield writer John Derry).

The Upper Derwent Valley Reservoirs are forever lodged in many memories as the training ground for 617 Squadron – 'The Dambusters' – in their modified Lancasters. The dams and reservoirs in this upland setting provided the perfect venue for 'dress-rehearsals' prior to the historic bombing runs over the Ruhr Valley. After the 'bouncing bomb' attacks on the Mohne Dam, fear of reprisals led to the erection of steel cables over the Derwent Valley Reservoirs and troops were brought in to man anti-aircraft gun installations. In May 1993, fifty years on from the tragic raid, thousands of people descended upon the Upper Derwent Valley to pay their respects and to witness the rare sight of a vintage Lancaster performing a low fly-past over the Dams: a fitting tribute to the men who courageously gave their lives in the daring mission (a memorial plaque, from the 1986 reunion, can be seen on the Derwent Dam).

Winter in Derwentdale (Paul Harrop)

Today, the waters and surrounding forests offer tranquillity to the visitor, although the popularity of the area means that the experience is usually shared with others. Yet the largely coniferous plantations and the artificial 'lakes' provide a valuable and relatively undisturbed habitat for some of Britain's rarest wildlife. Naturalists and conservationists who have tended to oppose all upland coniferous afforestation in the past are now in general agreement that the 'massed ranks' are not necessarily the wildlife deserts they were once thought to be: it should be clearly understood that the planting of alien conifers needs to be carefully planned if ecologically vital wildlife habitats and beautiful landscapes are to be protected but, whilst commercial plantations cannot support a diverse woodland aviifauna, the dense, mature forests of Derwentdale give cover to the scarce goshawk. Highly elusive in its phantom-like presence, this large, powerful raptor has recovered from the persecution which rendered the species extinct as a British breeding bird by the beginning of the 20th century. In the mid-1960s a nest was located and positively identified in a coniferous plantation in the Peak and it appears that this was a breeding attempt by escaped or released falcolners' goshawks. From such inauspicious beginnings a nucleus of wild breeding birds developed but, despite the protection of wardens and the law, the species continually faces threats from poisoning, shooting and the equally nauseating activities of egg-thieves or illegal falconers who mercilessly plunder the nests of these spectacular birds.

(Twitchers seeking a 'tick' should beware the fairly common female sparrowhawk, which is similar in appearance and hunting style to its *accipiter* cousin; but bear in mind that the larger, bulkier and more powerful goshawk preys on adult sparrowhawks, as well as juveniles.)

The Forestry Commission has endeavoured to protect the goshawk and its breeding sites throughout the country, and has managed to combine conservation with a policy of wide public access.

In early 1994, plans to privatise Forestry were shelved by the Government on the recommendations of the The Forestry Review Group; but, while wholesale privatisation was rejected, the piecemeal disposal of forests – including the sale of ancient woodland with SSSI status – to private owners is to be accelerated and the Forestry Commission to be made 'more business-like'. The Forestry Commission has come under a good deal of criticism as a 'timber factory' in the past, but there has been a more recent emphasis on conservation and access – neither of which are likely to be of concern to private owners, if past experience is anything to go by; the public has almost invariably been excluded from forests which have been flogged off under Government pressure. The effects of the creeping privatisation of forestry and woodland on Britain's wildlife and landscapes remain to be seen.

The Forestry Commission owns some 1,063 acres of forest, and native species are being planted to relieve the sometimes monotonous monoculture of the conifers – thus providing a more 'natural' and varied landscape which is of increasing benefit to the wildlife of the Peak National Park. The Severn-Trent Water Authority is another major landowner and much of the high moorland is now National Trust property; Officers from the landowning organisations, together with Peak Park Officers and representatives from local councils and other concerned bodies, form a joint group which co-ordinates the management and development of the Upper Derwent Valley, and the fruits of their labours are clear to see.

To control the plague of congestion, noise and air pollution caused by traffic, a mini-bus service is available to carry visitors between Fairholmes on the west bank of Ladybower and the King's Tree roundabout on summer Saturdays, Sundays and Bank Holiday Mondays, when the road is closed to other vehicles from Easter until the end of October. The road is also closed on Sundays from the beginning of November. The section of metalled road from Fairholmes to Mill Brook on the east side of Ladybower Reservoir is closed all year round, except to emergency or other essential services; disabled drivers may also use this section. Limited public transport is available along the A57 Snake Road to the Ladybower Inn (which lies east of Ashopton Viaduct and just off the Dark Peak Map), and to Fairholmes in Derwentdale – check for details. Some delightful approaches are possible from Bamford or Hope stations on the Hope Valley railway line – go via Win Hill for an especially scenic route.

Route 7(a):
Derwent Edge

Distance: 9 miles/14.5 km

Start: Ashopton Viaduct (SK 192864)

DERWENT Edge may be reached by divers means, the most popular being: from the Ladybower Inn which stands at the eastern foot of the Ladybower Reservoir (note the pub sign commemorating 'The Dambusters'); from Cutthroat Bridge further along the A57 Snake Road (car parking); from the Bradfield-Strines road east of the Edge; or from the Upper Derwent Valley, beneath the Edge. This is the northernmost section of the wonderful gritstone escarpment which dominates the Peak in the east and provides such a vital part of the National Park's unique character, but Derwent Edge appears more as a group of individual outcrops, rather than an uninterrupted 'edge' of millstone grit on the skyline, and the isolated outcrops and collections of rocks have intriguing titles: "The Wheel Stones" (or "Coach and Horses"); "The Salt Cellar"; "The Cakes o' Bread", are all worth a visit – and the views from Derwent Edge are spectacular. In this case, at least, the relative accessibility of the Edge gives the lie to that mindless maxim of the body fascists: "No pain, no gain".

THE ROUTE

FROM the layby at Ashopton Viaduct on the A57 Snake Road at Ladybower Reservoir, follow the bridleway heading north along the east side of the reservoir, passing the meagre detritus of Grainfoot Farm (a sacrifice to the mighty waters) to the metalled road and the inlet at Derwent, where only the name and a few submerged ruins remains of the little gritstone village. Continue on the quiet road beyond Mill Brook towards the magnificent 114 feet high Derwent Dam, before which the road loops to Fairholmes on the west side of the reservoirs. Your route lies along the track on the eastern side of Derwent Reservoir: where the road descends to the dam wall, take

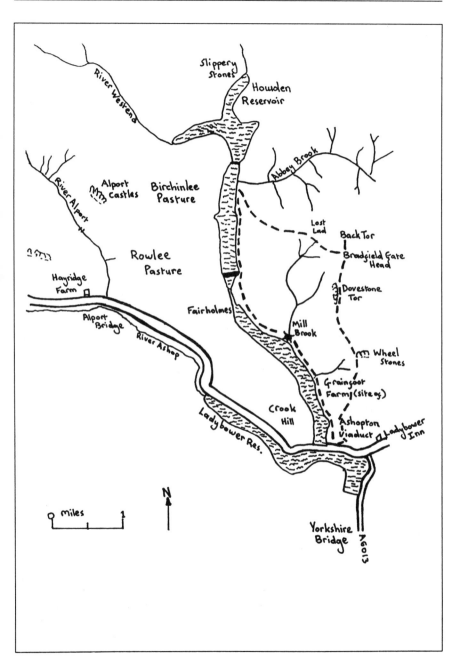

the track bearing right, to the east end of the Derwent Dam. (Alternatively, a little further along the road, at the bend, a path leads through the trees to join the track.)

Ladybower Reservoir from Whinstone Lee (Paul Harrop)

A gentle and delightful stroll beside Derwent Reservoir leads to the bottom of Abbey Brook and the track continues along the east bank of Howden Reservoir to Slippery Stones; however, to attain Derwent Edge you turn right before reaching Abbey Brook, along the path which puts the main Derwentdale track and the great sheet of water behind you as you ascend through Shireowlers North Plantation, over a stile next to a gate, and out onto Abbey Bank.

A path runs over rough grassland from Abbey Bank to Bradfield Gate Head and the ridge, where you turn left (ie. head north) to reach the isolated gritstone buttresses of Back Tor at a height of 1,765 feet/538 metres in a wild and romantic setting. As this is one of the less demanding routes in the book, pause for a while and absorb the views here and, even more inspiring, at Lost Lad: a wonderful vantage point which lies north-west of the summit of Back Tor – visitors will not be disappointed.

Head south from Back Tor and descend to the path over Derwent Edge, with a few patches of soggy ground to contend with after heavy rain. The first famous landmarks as you walk along the ridge of Derwent Edge are "The Cakes o' Bread"; (explanation would be superfluous). The excellent gritstone cliff of Dovestone Tor below the path is the focal point of Derwent Edge for rock climbers, and a cave here offers shelter (or a possible bivouac). Beyond Dovestone Tor is the 20 foot high boss of millstone grit known as "The Salt Cellar"; again, no explanation required.

The Wheel Stones (Paul Harrop)

Continuing along the Edge, over White Tor, you approach the prominent Wheel Stones or "The Coach and Horses" (the rocks resemble a coach and horses dashing along the skyline when viewed from the road below). Head south from these weathered stones – which are actually off the Dark Peak map, but this should not create any difficulty – then begin the descent from Derwent Edge via Whinstone Lee Tor and Lead Hill, down to Ashopton and the Ashopton Viaduct on the A57 Snake Road. The Ladybower Inn is a few yards east of Ashopton along the A57 – again just off the map – so those in need of immediate refreshment need not be alarmed.

Route 7 (b):
Abbey Brook, Howden Edge & Margery Hill

Distance: 12 miles/19 km

Start: Fairholmes, Derwentdale (SK 172892)

FAIRHOLMES, with its car park, picnic tables, refreshments, toilets, information centre (from which a useful leaflet may be obtained), cycle hire and mini-bus service, is the main base for exploring the Upper Derwent Valley, and there are several paths of the short, waymarked 'trail' variety in the vicinity. If this is not your 'scene', don't sneer: Derwentdale is something of a flagship of sustainable tourism for the Peak Park Authorities, the National Trust and the Forestry Commission, demonstrating how large numbers may be effectively managed through sensible traffic control; and many of the normally car-bound day-trippers who flock to the area are positively encouraged to cut the invisible umbilical which binds them to their vehicles – a tentative step, perhaps, towards a wider appreciation of the Peak's natural resources.

The following suggested route leaves this small outpost of civilisation behind, using it as a convenient springboard for a walk on the remote Howden Moors. Amongst the wildlife on the high ground of the eastern moors is a well-established colony of Mountain Hares – introduced from Scotland by 'sportsmen' during the last century – and, along with the inevitable red grouse and meadow pipits, waders and raptors might be seen. A cautionary note: crossing Abbey Brook after torrential rain can be an extremely necky exercise.

THE ROUTE

LEAVE Fairholmes by the main reservoir road heading north and turn right along the Mill Brook road (closed to traffic at all times) which loops below the Derwent Dam. After the bend, there is a footpath on your left which

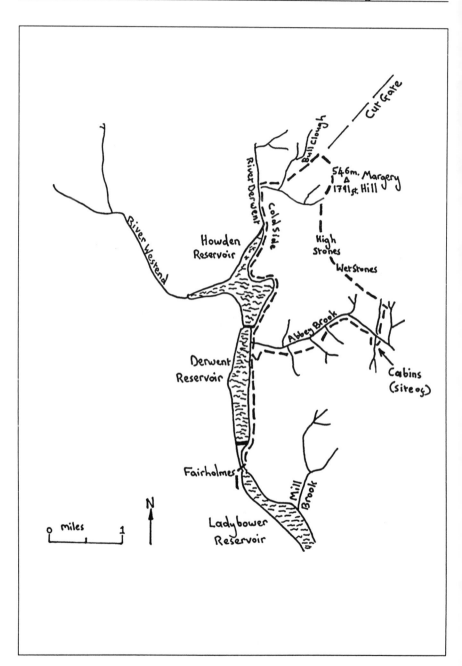

passes the east end of the Derwent Dam to deliver you through the trees to the track which runs along the east bank of the Derwent and Howden reservoirs.

Continue – as for the previous route – along the physically undemanding and aesthetically pleasing track to the Abbey Bank path, which begins near the Derbyshire/Yorkshire County Boundary, before the wide clough of Abbey Brook. Follow the path through the plantation in the direction of Abbey Bank until you ascend via the forest gate to the track on the south side of Abbey Brook. Stay on this clear track, past another gate and stile and over a clough which rifts Little Howden Moor, to Cogman Clough, the crossing of which involves a slight detour. After negotiating Cogman Clough, ascend gently past waterfalls and the gritstone crag of Berristers Tor – on your left, below Howden Edge – before the track bends south as you approach Sheepfold Clough. On your left, at the bottom of Sheepfold Clough and either side of the brook, may be seen the foundations and ruins of the old shooting cabins which once stood here.

Sheepfold Clough is easily forded near the cabin site. Once across the clough follow the path heading east for a short distance and keep a vigilant eye open for a path which forks to the left (north-east); follow this path on a descending traverse to Abbey Brook. Ford the stream and head north across the hillside, on an indistinct path, with Foul Clough to your left (west), then cross Foul Clough near its top. Your next objective is Wet Stones, which lie north-west of Foul Clough over pathless ground. At Wet Stones you may be relieved to know that the navigational difficulties are almost over. From the Wet Stones head north-west until you reach the path which runs north to Howden Edge, and follow this path along a channel to High Stones – at 1789 feet/546 metres, the highest point of Howden Edge. A superlative walk along the Edge awaits: follow the Edge path north, which provides easy going underfoot and uplifting panoramic vistas to your left (west), until you reach a junction above Wilfrey Edge where a path leads right (north) over Margery Hill, which reaches a summit height of 1791 feet/546 metres.

On July 21st, 1944, a Stirling bomber – LJ 628 of 1654 Heavy Conversion Unit, Wigsley – crashed at Grid reference 198954 on Upper Commons, to the east of Margery Hill, during a training exercise. The ten men on board were lucky to escape with their lives as the famously ungainly Stirling bumped over the moor: the rear turret was severed on impact (with its Rhodesian occupant, Rear gunner Sergeant Lennox van Nierkerk, still inside); the tail and short wings were ripped off; and the disproportionately elongated fuselage of the aircraft was broken in two. Bomb-aimer Sergeant Jim Coulson had to be cut from the wreckage with an axe, and he and the injured rear gunner were taken to Wharncliffe Hospital. Although both men required operations, they made excellent recoveries and continued their flying careers.

Further to the east is Broomhead Moor, scene of a recent flying tragedy. With all-round improvements in aviation equipment, aircraft crashes on the Dark Peak moors are rare; but on 11th June, 1993, a restored Hawker Hunter fighter trainer *en route* to the Blackpool air show smashed into Broomhead Moor whilst flying in bad weather; the aircraft hit the desolate moorland at an estimated speed of 450 mph. A search for wreckage and the remains of the experienced pilot took two weeks.

To the north of Margery Hill, at grid reference 186965, a shallow crater (which has now filled with water) on Featherbed Moss marks the blast site of a German V1 'Flying Bomb' which fell short of Manchester; fragments of the aluminium bomb casing have been found at this site.

To continue with the route: press on from the summit of Margery Hill, north-west to the Cut Gate path. Turn left and stick with the distinctive path, descending between Bull Clough to your right and Cranberry Clough to your left. The Cut Gate path eventually crosses Bull Clough near its confluence with Cranberry Clough beyond which is the footbridge, which you cross: from this point you may either follow the track via Cold Side and continue along the east bank of Howden Reservoir to the Howden Dam and on alongside Derwent Reservoir to the Derwent Dam and Fairholmes; or, if the mini-bus is operating, take the path which forks right from the track a few yards south of the footbridge which will bring you to the packhorse bridge at Slippery Stones – cross the historic bridge and follow the path south along the west bank of Howden Reservoir to King's Tree or West End and enjoy a ride back to Fairholmes. (You could of course return on foot via the west bank of Howden Reservoir, but walking around the Fox's Piece inlet, west to West End then east to the main 'body' of Howden, calls for iron resolve.)

Route 7 (c):
Bull Stones, Crow Stones &
Shepherds' Meeting Stones

Distance: 10.5 miles / 17 km

Start: King's Tree. (SK 168939)

KING'S Tree is the end of the line on the west bank of Howden, and on those occasions when the road north from Fairholmes is closed to motor vehicles it may be reached by the mini-bus which turns at the Howden roundabout, just before Linch Clough.

The Howden Moors, separated from the bulk of Bleaklow by the River Derwent, form a ridge which provides highly rewarding walking in a beautiful landscape. In spring and summer, listen for the evocative call of the curlew and the piping of the golden plover; from late autumn to early spring, hen harriers might be seen – the Eastern moors regularly hold over-wintering hen harriers (a major roost is on Broomhead Moor, east of Margery Hill), and summering birds have occurred. Widespread illegal (and unjustifiable) persecution, loss of moorland habitat and the activities of egg-thieves have all contributed to the serious decline of this lovely raptor, but with luck you may witness the birds quartering the moors as they hunt for prey, or see them in buoyant flight over the Upper Derwent Valley.

THE ROUTE

FROM the end of the road at King's Tree follow the clear track north over the Linch Clough stepping stones and continue through the forestry plantation to the path which delivers you to the packhorse bridge at Slippery Stones. Across the bridge, you take the footpath to the footbridge over the

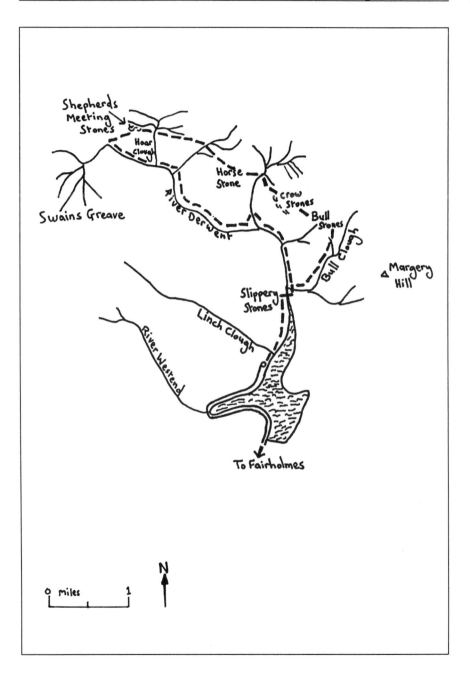

brook of Cranberry Clough; cross this and bear right (east) on the Cut Gate path.

Just before the crossing of the lively little stream which runs through Bull Clough, turn left and pursue the sketchy path which runs north-east from the clear Cut Gate route along Bull Clough (to your right) and descends to the stream; some rock-hopping and crossing of banks may be required as you make your way through the clough to the Bull Stones, on the hillside at the head of Bull Clough.

Pause and enjoy the distant views for a moment then head north-west over the heather on an intermittent path to the Crow Stones, via Broadhead Clough Head.

On April 12th, 1951 a converted light civil transport aircraft, Consul TF-RPM, crashed at Grid Reference 177966 near the head of Broadhead Clough – forty miles east of the planned course. The 'plane was flying from Croyden to Iceland, via Liverpool and Prestwick, but was forced off-course by high winds and crashed whilst flying blind in low cloud. The crashed Consul and the bodies of the three men on board were discovered by a Sheffield rambler on Crow Stone Edge. A few items of wreckage may still be seen today as you cross Broadhead Clough Head.

Another crash site lies approximately half a mile to the east, at Grid Reference 184967 on Featherbed Moss. Oxford LX 518 crashed into the moor here on 19th October, 1943 – after drifting some forty miles off-course in bad weather during a night training exercise – killing the pilot on impact. The wreckage was not discovered until October 23rd.

At the eroded Crow Stones and the Rocking Stone on Crow Stones Edge the far-ranging panorama provides a truly uplifting experience, with the Holme Moss transmitter offering the only tangible sign of modern human activity. This is a superb spot for a comprehensive appreciation of the magnificent Bleaklow massif, weather conditions permitting, and the haunting sounds of the moorland birds provide the only appropriate sound-track to compliment the glorious vista. There are, fortunately, still some experiences that cannot be packaged, price-tagged and 'marketed'.

A pleasant return to the Upper Derwent Valley may be made down the hillside by Broadhead Clough if desired, but the present suggested route continues on high ground for a while longer: your way lies north from Crow Stones Edge to the waterfall in Stainery Clough – below the dreaded groughs of Stainery Clough Head – where you bear left (west) to the Horse Stone on Horse Stone Naze. The Stone itself may not be much to look at, but the wild setting stirs the spirit. From Horse Stone Naze, head north-west towards Coldwell Clough: a little persistence may be necessary as you negotiate Coldwell Clough Head to achieve your next objective, the lonely Shepherd's Meeting Stones above Hoar Clough – but the effort will be rewarded. Make your way west from Coldwell Clough over some peaty terrain to reach the top of Hoar Clough and the edge path to Shepherd's Meeting Stones.

(If the weather is good and your fitness not in question, Bleaklow may beckon: a worthwhile route to the Barrow Stones – visible over the valley from Shepherd's Meeting Stones – can be made west via Dean Head to Swain's Head, then around Swain's Greave to the Barrow Stones and the main Bleaklow ridge.)

To return to the valley now: either walk east a few yards to Hoar Clough and descend along the east bank; or head west over Dean Head to the River Derwent,then east along the north bank of the river. Note Barrow Clough on your right – which provides a direct ascent to Barrow Stones and the main Bleaklow ridge – as you approach the bottom of Hoar Clough. Cross Hoar Clough and Coldwell Clough (the upper path hereabouts is the driest option after wet weather) and continue alongside the winding river by Humber Knoll, over Lands Clough where the clear track running along Lands Side commences. This track delivers you to Slippery Stones, the only real potential difficulty being the crossing of Stainery Clough – which can be a desperate affair after persistent rainfall.

Once you have forded Stainery Clough, the footbridge over Cranberry Clough is easily reached and shortly after crossing the footbridge a path on your right leads you to the packhorse bridge, which you cross to the forest path on the west side of the River Derwent and Howden Reservoir; walk pleasantly through the plantation to King's Tree, the end of the reservoir road and the end of this suggested route. If you are waiting for the mini-bus, enjoy the views over Howden and keep an eye out for waterfowl and other birds.

The artificial lakes of Howden, Derwent and Ladybower are relatively species-poor, being steep-sided and lacking in the mud and shallows favoured by waders and water birds, but red-breasted mergansers and teal have bred here, and the banks of the reservoirs provide valuable nesting sites for sandpipers. Cormorants are fairly regularly seen, and a much less common visitor is sometimes recorded on spring or autumn passage: the scarce osprey. For a few days in June 1977, an osprey was regularly seen fishing the reservoirs before it finally moved on, and sporadic sightings of this rare raptor have been made in various years.

The forests cloaking the reservoirs hold flocks of the diminutive and extremely active goldcrest – Britain's smallest bird – which may be seen (or heard) high in the trees. Crossbills breed here and siskins, redpolls, jays, wrens and robins are 'regulars', whilst tawny owls can be found in the mature plantations. Younger, dense coniferous plantations attract long-eared owls and short-eared owls – the latter may sometimes be seen quartering the moors, harrier-like, during the daylight hours. Yellowhammers, reed bunting, warblers and whinchats frequent the young coniferous plantations and woodpigeon are abundant throughout Derwentdale. Of the woodland mammals the grey squirrel is common, although the red squirrel might be seen in the quieter regions. Pine martens are reputed to haunt the forests (although few people have actually seen them). Green hairstreak butterflies may be seen, particularly around Ladybower, and all in all, the effects of the reservoirs and the extensive upland afforestation on the Peak's wildlife – and the landscape – cannot be described as wholly detrimental.

The hand of man has been rather less successful in Longdendale, but Crowden still provides an excellent valley base for exploring Bleaklow to the south and Black Hill to the north. Some punters argue that you haven't really been bogtrotting until you've traversed the (allegedly) cruel summit of Black Hill (which isn't strictly true, but try it anyway – you might even enjoy the experience).

8

LONGDENDALE

THE valley of the Uppper Etherow – described as 'waste' in the Domesday Book – once formed the boundary of the jealously guarded hunting territory of successive mediaeval monarchs: The Royal Forest of the Peak, an area of some forty square miles, harshly administered from Peveril Castle at Castleton. (Whether the valley was laid waste as part of the bloody 'pacification' of the north carried out by William the Conqueror or a peaceful migration from the small settlements of Crowden and Woodhead to the lowlands is not known.)

The monks of Charlesworth were amongst those who farmed the wild valley, and woodland was cleared as sheep grazing took priority in Longdendale and environs. In the 17th century, the road from Cheshire through Longdendale to Yorkshire (turnpiked in 1731) heralded a new era of transport, whilst the arrival of the cotton trade in Tintwhistle, *circa* 1750, and its subsequent expansion throughout the nineteenth century, transformed the tiny village into a hive of mill-based industry, powered by the River Etherow. With the later decline of the cotton business the mills closed and the population of Tintwhistle fell.

Many of the mills disappeared under the waters of the Longdendale reservoirs, completed in 1877. Work began on the reservoirs of Bottoms, Valehouse, Rhodeswood, Torside and Woodhead in 1848, following the completion of the first Woodhead railway tunnel. This ambitious feat of railway engineering had exacted a dreadful toll as many navigators were killed or seriously injured whilst labouring under obscene conditions; a second tunnel, completed in 1852, resulted in more deaths as cholera spread throughout the navvies' community. The first two tunnels were closed – the second of the tunnels now carries power lines – when the third tunnel was opened and an electrified line installed. The Trans-Pennine passenger route operated until 1970, and the line was closed completely in 1981. Part of the track-bed is now the Longdendale Trail, which offers some easy walking and cycling opportunities.

Descending to Crowden (Paul Harrop)

Tintwhistle and the northern part of Longdendale was once part of Cheshire, but local government reorganisation transferred the area to Derbyshire in 1974.

Longdendale has been spared (for the present) the oft-proposed Trans-Pennine motorway, but the existing major road, the obvious reservoirs and the ugly transmission lines and pylons scar the area, spoiling what should be a beautiful valley by creating the impression of an industrial site whose industry has fled. The existence of these blots on the landscape has not gone unnoticed by the road-building lobby who argue that, since Longdendale has already been marred, a motorway would not make much difference (as the late Eric Morecambe used so famously to say: "There's no answer to that!") Yet, when the sun shines over the brightly coloured yachts on

Torside Reservoir, the valley is not completely without charm; and there is no doubt as to its value as a 'base camp' for high moorland walking.

Crowden is the usual centre of operations, with its car-park, youth hostel and camp-site. Easily accessible from Manchester and Sheffield by private transport, public transport is also available along the A628, although at least one service has been axed – a victim of deregulation. The National Express service 350 currently stops at Crowden-in-Longdendale and a Mainline service (402) operates under contract to the Peak Park Joint Planning Board on summer Sundays and Bank Holiday Mondays (as always, check for bus times and details).

Route 8(a):
Black Hill

Distance: 10 miles/16 km

Start: Crowden Youth Hostel, Crowden (SK 073993)

CROWDEN Youth Hostel stands on the north side of the A628 Manchester-Barnsley road, overlooking Torside Reservoir; a car and coach-park adjoins the main road nearby, and there is an excellent camp-site which gives priority to backpackers. The hostel was converted from a row of six railwaymen's cottages on the initiative of the Peak Park Planning Board and opened in the summer of 1965. This being a National Park hostel it is open to all, and YHA membership is not a necessary prerequisite (but YHA members pay YHA prices). Both the hostel and camp-site have provided overnight accommodation for countless Pennine Wayfarers, and pre-booking is advisable. The lack of a nearby pub might, however, deter some from extending their stay in the valley.

Much has been written about the squelchy nature of Black Hill: most famously, the late Alfred Wainwright recalled that he once sank almost up to his knees whilst negotiating a particularly evil trough of peat, and only the combined tuggings of his companion and a conveniently-placed Park Ranger – who says you can never find one when you need one? – could extricate the distressed (and overweight) fellwalker. Wainwright – "Blessed be the solitary walker" – was sufficiently perturbed by the memory to suggest that a strong-armed companion should be included on any trek over this treacherous hill.

There can be no doubt that the glutinous peat can make for very heavy going, but when the ground freezes in winter walking on the plateau may be less gruelling. The landscape, however, is bleak at any time of the year. Mist often descends quickly on Black Hill. The BBC Holme Moss Transmitter, standing on the Yorkshire border, can be an invaluable landmark: the Holme Moss television station is situated just off the A6024, the nearest road to the Black Hill plateau and a possible escape route in dire conditions. In real emergency, assistance may be obtained from the Mountain Rescue Post at Crowden.

The descent from Black Hill (Paul Harrop)

THE ROUTE

AT the hostel, follow the lane, bearing left over Crowden Brook, and continue until the Pennine Way signpost points your clear route to Laddow Rocks. Alternatively, from the rear of the car park head for the (signposted) toilets and turn right by the camp-site to the lane; cross the stile ahead, beside the Crowden Outdoor Centre gate – Private Road and Fire Access – and continue, crossing the brook, along the concessionary path beside the Outdoor Centre and onto the Pennine Way route for Laddow Rocks.

The Pennine Way gently climbs north-north-west towards the gritstone crags of Laddow, with Crowden Great Brook coursing below to your right. Stay with the Pennine Way path, crossing Oakenclough Brook before ascending to the top of the ridge. (An alternative path continues below Laddow Rocks, but the high route offers wider views.)

At the moorland edge, bear right to a fork in the path marked by a cairn on the top of Laddow Rocks: the left fork leads to Greenfield via Chew Reservoir, the Chew Valley and Dove Stone Reservoir. Take the right fork and continue to the end of the outcrop.

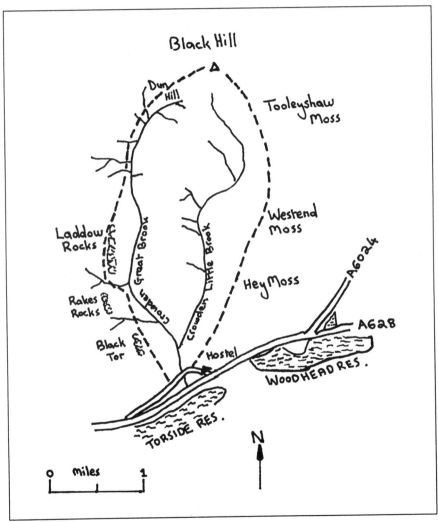

A climbing accident at Laddow Rocks in 1923 led to serious thought being given to the problems posed by evacuation of injured parties from the crags. After a dreadful fall down Green Gully, Edgar Pryor was carried from the moor on a 'stretcher' hurriedly manufactured from two 'wooden liars' – the 'No Trespass' signs had some use, after all – but despite the best efforts of Wilson Hey, surgeon and fellow Rucksack Club member, Pryor eventually needed a paralysed leg amputated. Hey immediately proposed a Stretcher-Sub-Committee, which was set up to examine practical designs for stretchers and to suggest general improvements in rescue and first-aid equipment. Eustace Thomas (a bogtrotter of some repute after completing the Derwent Watershed), helped in the design of the Thomas Stretcher and Wilson Hey developed a standard medical kit – unfortunately, Hey was fined by the Home Office, who objected to his provision of morphia for victims of accidents in the hills. Nevertheless, from humble beginnings an effective and coordinated Mountain Rescue Service has evolved, with a network of seven teams covering the whole of the Peak National Park – for particularly difficult evacuations, RAF helicopters may be employed to airlift casualties to safety.

Laddow Rocks has declined in popularity as a climbing ground, despite the undoubted quality of many of the routes to be found here. It seems that many climbers today tend to spurn the 'long walk-in' to the more isolated crags – a situation which suits the 'traditionalist' who prefers to climb far from the Stanage crowds. A rake at the end of the crag leads to the base of the first buttress, where a cave provides a rare chance for shelter and a possible bivouac. The 'Cave Crack' which takes the overhang forming the roof of the cave was first climbed by the remarkable Norwegian cragsman Ivar Berg in June 1916. Berg audaciously ascended the route solo, in clogs, before turning his attention to the 'Cave Arete' which he climbed in similar style; although he did remove his jacket before making the first ascent of the arete.

After Laddow Rocks the paths above and below the outcrop merge and the valley opens out as you follow Crowden Brook upstream to the confluence with Meadowgrain Clough. Ascend north-east over the morass of Grains Moss and Dun Hill, crossing the Derbyshire/Yorkshire border, where marshy ground and cotton-grass surrenders to the soft blanket of black, wind-blown peat. The area resembles a popular conception of a moonscape; except explorers here have the force of gravity to contend with. Ahead, a white beacon amidst the over-grazed and acid-rain drenched desolation, stands the triangulation pillar marking the summit of the aptly-named Black Hill, at a height of 1908 feet/582 metres.

> The elemental top is known as 'Soldier's Lump': a reference to the triangulation party of the Corps of Royal Engineers who constructed the column. The inhospitable 'Lump' is no place to linger, and it takes no great imaginative leap to guess the sentiments expressed by the surveyors as they carried out their work here. It is possible, and in extremely wet conditions eminently sensible, to skirt the worst of the summit muck by steering clear of the triangulation point altogether; purists will, of course, bash on regardless – but even Leopold von Sacher-Masoch himself would have been hard pressed to derive anything resembling 'pleasure' from the experience of crossing the boggiest stretch of Black Hill. (The pillar itself stands on a tiny island of dry ground, which you may be loath to leave.)

The return to Crowden keeps to high ground for most of the way and there are some rewarding views to be had, given good visibility. From the summit column – or as close as you dare get to it – head south-south-east over Tooleyshaw Moss (the cairns provide assistance and reassurance, if needed, and the Holme Moss transmitter provides further guidance.) There is still some soggy terrain over Tooleyshaw Moss, but this is as nothing when compared with the oozing wasteland you have left behind.

Gradually bear south along the descending ridge of Tooleyshaw Moor and cross White Low, then head south-south-west up to Westend Moss. To the south is the Bleaklow massif and the main Bleaklow ridge; often lying beneath a gathering bank of cumulus or malevolent cumulo-nimbus cloud.

Descend from Westend Moss, bearing right over Hey Moss, then drop down to the hostel lane by descending the hillside on a clear path between the disused Brockholes and Loftend quarries, crossing the Boundary of Access Land to emerge at Crowden. After the stark and forbidding summit, the apocalyptic vision of the utility pylons and the thundering of the traffic along the A628 might induce a sense of shock; some small consolation might be taken from the knowledge that at least the motorway builders have so far been foiled in their plans to completely destroy this already despoiled valley forever.

Route 8(b):
Torside Clough, The Bleaklow Ridge &
Far Black Clough

Distance: 11.5 miles/18.5 km

Start: Crowden Car Park, Crowden (SK 074994)

THE Pennine Way crosses Longdendale beside Torside Reservoir, providing a convenient route from the valley to the main Bleaklow ridge via Torside Clough. The Longdendale reservoir chain lacks the aesthetic appeal of the Upper Derwent Valley, but the waters still provide habitat for several species of birds: breeding teal, little ringed plovers, black headed gulls, sandpipers and herons are regularly seen; rare passage migrants – including the splendid osprey – sometimes occur in the valley, and in 1982 a golden eagle was seen in the area. The hills around the valley hold breeding short-eared owls, which prey mostly on short-tailed voles; thus, the number of owls in any year is closely related to the density of the vole population in the vicinity.

THE ROUTE

LEAVE the car-park for the lane and bear left along it, continuing to the main (A628) road. Walk down the road until you can cross to Hollins and the dam at the west end of Torside Reservoir; the reservoir is often delightfully dotted with yachts from the Glossop Sailing Club. Go over the dam to reach the trackbed of the old railway and the Torside Crossing. (To your left, east along the Longdendale Trail and just below it, is a car-park – an alternative starting and finishing point for motorists doing this walk – a National Park information centre, picnic area and toilets.)

Follow the path to Torside Clough, cross the stream and continue along the Pennine Way ascending – with Torside Clough to your left – onto Clough Edge. Some bog-trotting is required near Torside Castle as you

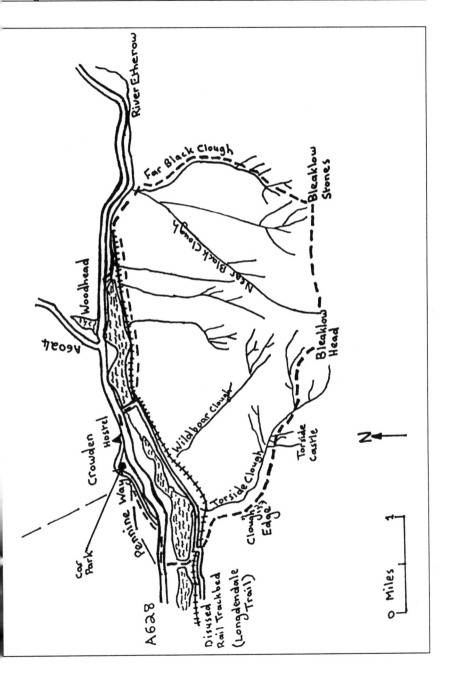

approach Wildboar Grain and the spring known as John Track Well, at the head of the stream which flows through Torside Clough. You must now follow Wildboar Grain around onto Far Moss, finally bearing south for Bleaklow Head where you may enjoy a brief respite from the peat.

Head east over the ridge via Bleaklow Hill to Bleaklow Stones, with stakes and poles to assist you on the journey through the worst of Bleaklow's groughs.

On attaining the Bleaklow Stones – which is in itself no mean feat in bad weather – make your way north-east into the head-waters of Far Black Clough, picking up a path as you descend quite pleasantly, dropping down into the clough where you eventually join a clear shooters' track leading to the Longdendale Trail.

Turn left (west) and walk along the Trail beside Woodhead Reservoir to the east end of Torside Reservoir, where a track leads to the A628 and Crowden. (Bear in mind that crossing the road can be the riskiest part of a moorland walk.)

On 5th December, 1956, a USAF L-20 A Beaver crashed at Grid Reference 056976 on Bramagh Edge, west of Torside Clough and overlooking Torside and Rhodeswood Reservoirs. Pilot error, bad weather, misidentification by ground control and the faults of early radio-navigation equipment conspired to bring the single-engined aircraft to a point twenty-five miles off-course; and a tragic end. The crash and subsequent fire was witnessed by a signalman at Torside, who alerted the emergency services; but sadly there was nothing to be done for the pilot and passenger. Today, navigational equipment has improved tremendously; which is just as well, considering the number of low-flying airliners regularly seen over Black Hill and Laddow as they approach Manchester.

9

SADDLEWORTH - CHEW VALLEY

THE Saddleworth Moors provide some excellent and challenging high-level routes (see following chapter *The Big Walks*). The routes described here are completely covered by the Dark Peak Outdoor Leisure Map, although the OS. 1:25 000 sheet SE 00 (Saddleworth Moor) might prove to be useful.

Many ramblers' experience of the Saddleworth Moors is limited to the original Pennine Way crossing of the wet, peaty, White Moss and Black Moss, north-west over the moor from the A635 'Isle Of Skye' road (off the Dark Peak map) to the Standedge cutting. This may give rather a poor impression, particularly in bad weather (most Pennine Wayfarers prefer the 'Wessenden Alternative' – now the 'Official' route – to the east, which goes via Wessenden Head and Wessenden Reservoir to Black Moss). There are many local bogtrotters who will testify to the rewards of wider exploration, and the area of the Saddleworth Moors covered by the Dark Peak map has much to offer. Similarly, the Chew Valley will undoubtedly repay the visitor. The superb gritstone crags – Dovestones, Raven Stones, Raven Stones Quarry, Wilderness Rocks and the magnificent Winberry, amongst others – have seen a resurgence of interest from climbers; from the 1940s to the 1960s this was one of the most popular climbing areas in the Peak, but rumours of the long walk-ins (encouraged by local cragsmen?) deterred modern rock-jocks for years. Wilderness Gully in the Chew Valley has sad associations for many climbers; the renowned Chew Valley Cragsmen – and pioneers of Derbyshire limestone climbing – Graham West and Michael Roberts, lost their lives in an avalanche here in 1963.

The edges provide superb walking opportunities, with expansive views and a real feeling of open space; buzzards are occasionally seen in the Saddleworth-Chew region, usually on passage – although birds have wintered on the Dark Peak moors. Buzzards soar and glide on broad, 'fingered'

Holme Moss transmitter: landmark in the peak desert (Paul Harrop)

wings – "the tourists' eagle", the hillmen of Scotland call them, although the golden eagle is much larger – and emits a mewing call. Unfortunately, the birds are still unjustifiably persecuted, and birds are regularly poisoned, trapped and shot by gamekeepers and farmers throughout England, Scotland and Wales.

Kestrels are well-established throughout the Peak, although the species did not completely escape the effects of extensive pesticide use in the 1950s and 1960s. (In 1939 a Swiss chemist, Paul Mueller, discovered the first organochlorine pesticide, DDT, and was awarded a Nobel prize for it in 1948. Today, it is banned throughout much of the world because of its devastating effects on the environment; a salutary tale for those whose blind faith in science leads them to believe the bland reassurances of 'experts' in white coats.)

The following suggestions offer an 'on the edge' walk with delightful gritstone scenery and, in contrast, a more committing bout of bogtrotting over the moorland interior.

Route 9(a):
Raven Stones

Distance: 8 miles/13 km

Start: Dove Stone Reservoir (SE 014034)

THE gritstone edges overlooking the triple chain of Dove Stone, Yeoman Hey and Greenfield Reservoirs provide a splendid promenade with expansive views, all within easy reach of Greenfield and the A635 'Isle Of Skye' road. Greenfield is served by bus and rail; but check for services and times. Motorists can find parking and toilet facilities situated at the south-west corner of Dove Stone Reservoir, where there is a Mountain Rescue Post and Warden Briefing Centre (manned at weekends only) in case of emergency.

THE ROUTE

FROM the Dove Stone Reservoir car-park, follow the Dove Stone dam north and turn right at the end of the wall. Continue along the path to the reservoir road and the Yeoman Hey dam.

At the south-west corner of Yeoman Hey Reservoir take the track running along the western side of the reservoir to Greenfield Reservoir. As you approach the latter, Greenfield Brook is to your right and the curiously-named 'Bill o' Jacks' Plantation stands to your left.

> The name of the plantation derives from one Bill Bradbury – Bill o' Jacks' – a local gamekeeper and landlord at the 'Moorcock Inn', which stood on the main A628 road north of Binn Green. In April 1832, Bill Bradbury and his son Thomas were found murdered at the Moorcock Inn, and the finger of suspicion pointed directly at two poachers against whom the now terminally-silenced Bradburys had been due to testify. The known poachers were tried for the murders, but were acquitted due to lack of solid evidence; the case remains unsolved.

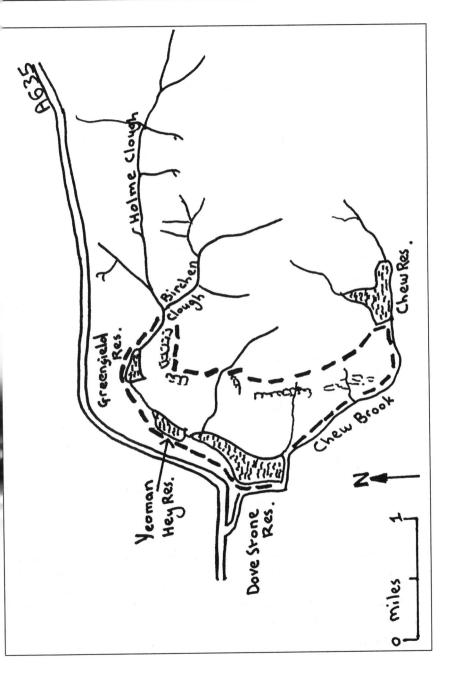

Walk alongside Greenfield Reservoir and beyond, up through the valley in the company of the delightful Greenfield Brook, with the black gritstone outcrop of Raven Stones high above to your right, until you reach the confluence of Holme Clough and Birchen Clough below Raven Stones Brow.

Holme Clough may be reached via the iron ladder; your present route, however, takes the easier but equally worthwhile right-hand fork of Birchen Clough, past the Dove Stone tunnel and on along the course of the rocky, narrowing defile. Astute boulder-hopping may be in order and particular care should be exercised after heavy rain, when a closer acquaintance with the brook becomes alarmingly likely. Make your way through Birchen Clough until a short ascent right (west) brings you to the path – clearly marked on the map and well-defined on the ground – running along the gritstone edge of Raven Stones. A pleasing stroll along the top of the crags brings you to the most famous feature of Raven Stones: The Trinnacle. The top(s) of this split gritstone pinnacle may be reached by a 'moderate' route, via the 'back and foot' chimney; whilst the 'Trinnacle East' provides more of a challenge, at a 'Very Severe' grade, for competent parties.

Follow the edge path towards Ashway Rocks, then head south-south-west to the Ashway Stone on Ashway Moss. Near the Ashway Stone stands the Platt Memorial, where James Platt, Member of Parliament for Oldham, died in a shooting accident in 1857. Beyond the memorial, cross Dovestone Clough and press on above Dove Stones Edge and Dove Stones Quarries, which provide excellent climbing; the Main Quarry routes are longer than is usual for gritstone, and even today many of the lines have an air of seriousness about them.

> Of interest to the aviation archaeologist is the nearby Dean Rocks, the scene of a Mosquito aircraft crash, and Charnel Clough to the south, reputedly the crash site of a Messerschmitt.

To the west of Dove Stones Edge, at Grid Reference 041033 on Slate Pit Moss, a Lysander (V9403) of 6 Anti-Aircraft Co-operation unit crashed whilst flying to Rhyl from Ringway on 19th August 1941. A fault with the directional gyro sent the Lysander on a wrong heading; into the low cloud and high ground of the Peak.

From Dove Stone Edge and Quarries (Great Dove Stone Rocks and Little

Dove Stone Rocks) make for the enigmatic Bramley's Cot, then follow the moorland rim towards Dish Stone Rocks then bear left to the dam wall at the west end of Chew Reservoir, from where an undemanding two-mile return may be made via the reservoir road running roughly alongside Chew Brook through the Chew Valley to Dove Stone Reservoir.

Route 9(b):
Holme Clough, Black Hill &
Chew Reservoir

Distance: 13.5 miles/22 km

Start: Binn Green (SE 018044)

THE Binn Green Picnic Area lies barely within the Peak, near the point where the National Park Boundary crosses the A635 Holmefirth road approximately one mile east of Greenfield. The site, with its car park, toilets and picnic tables, is popular with the summer weekend and Bank Holiday crowds who flock to the reservoirs at the merest hint of good weather; an early arrival is advisable at such times.

Holme Clough actually lies outside of Access land – thus, the description of the following route does not imply that ramblers have the right to be there.

THE ROUTE

FROM the picnic area, attain the reservoir road via the steps and the coniferous plantation. At the stile, follow the road left to the dam wall at the southern end of Yeoman Hey Reservoir and continue as for the previous route up through the valley, past Greenfield Reservoir and along Greenfield Brook to the Holme Clough/Birchen Clough junction beneath the black crags of Raven Stones.

Gain Holme Clough via the ladder and continue along the left bank of the brook as far as the confluence with Rimmon Pit Clough, on your left. Ascend Rimmon Pit Clough, progressing (with due care and attention) along the rocky bed of the shallow watercourse and up onto moorland of particularly grim repute: to the west and north-west, Sail Bark Moss and Hollin Brown Knoll (which is just off the Dark Peak map) are embedded in

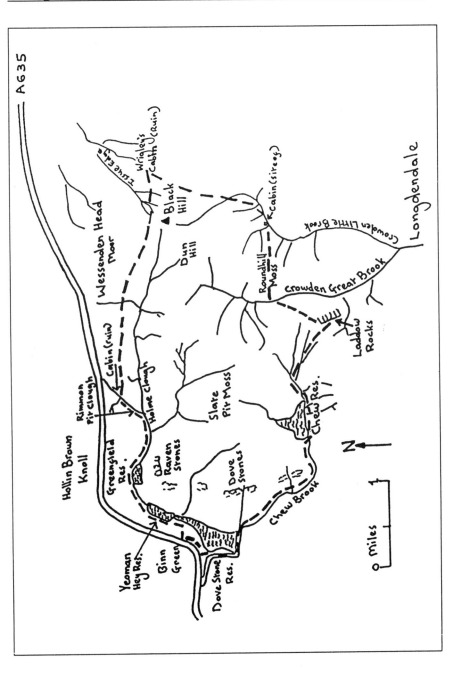

the yellow-press fed public consciousness, due to associations with the Moors Murders investigations and the notorious trial in 1966.

Leave Rimmon Pit Clough at the old cabin which stands at the fork in the stream (grid reference 043057) and head east over Little Moss. Gradually bear right into Holme Clough and continue to the original Pennine Way route. Summit baggers and masochists may head for the triangulation pillar on Black Hill, whilst those who have experienced the dubious delights of a visit to 'Soldier's Lump' should forge ahead over unremitting terrain to the ruined Wrigley's Cabin (at grid reference 084051) at Great Hill on Issue Edge, where a welcome rest may be taken in preparation for the next stage. Enjoy the birds for a while.

Crossing the Black Hill plateau (Paul Harrop)

Meadow pipits are almost an integral part of the scene on moorland walks in the Dark Peak, and its faint, high-pitched cheep may be heard almost everywhere, although the sound is sometimes carried away by the moorland winds. In spring and early summer, watch out for the entertaining 'all-singing, all parachuting' display made by the males as part of their courting ritual. The skylark is similar in appearance and 'jizz', but the bulky shape and the head-crest of the latter should distinguish the species; in display, the skylark hovers whilst it sings, in contrast to the 'parachute' descent of the meadow pipit.

The most important moorland bird in many ways is, of course, the unmis-takeable red grouse. Its variety of calls – including the characteristic 'go-back, go-back' – regularly and unexpectedly breaks the silence of the moors. Ramblers may often flush a bird from cover, and the grouse then demonstrates its ability to fly with surprising strength and purpose for such a dumpy creature; hence their value to the field-sportsman. Given the managed habitat, red grouse might be seen as the ultimate free-range bird; after all, whilst 'blood sports' raise fierce emotions, game birds do not suffer the abject horror which faces that other free-roaming source of food, sheep and lambs, as they go to the slaughter-house.

Almost two miles south-west of Great Hill and one and a half miles south of the triangulation pillar on the summit of Black Hill is the site of another ruined cabin, near the confluence of Meadow Clough and Crowden Little Brook below Crowden Meadows. Although the distance may not be great, the going can be excruciating over the Black Hill plateau. The Holme Moss transmitter provides an aid to navigation as you negotiate the peaty wastes.

The hut which once stood here was deliberately razed to the ground by a lackey of the Manchester Water Board in the mid-1960s; the Board objected to ramblers taking shelter here, and in a mood of sheer spite they ordered that the cabin be burned down.

From the cabin site, head west over the barren Roundhill Moss to Crowden Great Brook, which you must cross to reach the Pennine Way at a point approximately half a mile north-east of Laddow Rocks. Follow the Pennine Way over Laddow Rocks, keeping an eye out for the path which heads north-west from the top of Laddow, over Laddow Moss to Chew Clough and the east end of Chew Reservoir. Stay with the path down to Chew Reservoir and continue along the southern bank to the south-western extremity of the reservoir. At this point you turn right towards Chew Mount (*not* along the Chew dam wall, which would deliver you onto Chew Moss) then left at Chew Mount – passing the southern end of the gritstone crags of Dishstone Rocks with Chew Brook on your left. Continue easily, keeping Chew Brook to your left, over the bottom of Charnel Clough and on below Charnel Holes; keep to the main track, and cross Chew Brook to the southern end of Dove Stone Reservoir, and continue to the Dove Stone dam. Walk along the wall and turn right at its end; follow the path right, and proceed with ease to the 'Isle of Skye' road and the Binn Green car-park.

Laddow Rocks (Paul Harrop)

10

THE BIG WALKS

A long tradition of hard moorland walking has been well maintained in the Dark Peak, and the expansion of interest in challenging walks led to the foundation in 1972 of the Long Distance Walker's Association, which now holds a database of information on routes over 20 miles throughout Britain (including Northern Ireland). There are as many reasons for attempting a long distance walk as there are ramblers: there are 'challenge' badge and certificate collectors; 'new route' seekers; fitness freaks and would-be 're-cord breakers'; and walkers who simply enjoy the occasional hard day out. Whatever your particular 'bag', the following routes should provide an enjoyable adventure on the Dark Peak moors and environs. No badges or certificates are available for these particular routes; those desirous of tangible rewards should check out the numerous organised and 'anytime' challenge walks, of which the Long Distance Walkers Association has a comprehensive list and full details.

Marsden-Edale

THIS 25 mile (approximately) route is *the* classic walk of the Dark Peak. The OS. Sheet Number 110 (Sheffield & Huddersfield) 1:50,000 will be required as this covers the whole of the route, but the Dark Peak map is invaluable for most of the walk. The route and time taken can be varied to suit individual tastes, abilities and ambitions.

The Marsden-Edale route was developed by Cecil Dawson, who named Ross Evans as the true founder of the route, during the early 1900s. Hard men and women might attempt to go for 'the double', first completed by Fred Heardman, in the 1920s. If a leisurely approach is favoured, then the

Crowden camp-site or hostel provides a convenient overnight stop. The Pennine Way (original or alternative) can be followed over the moors or a more direct line taken, but generally the route is as follows:

MARSDEN – Blakely and Wessenden Reservoirs; Wessenden Head (A635); Black Hill; Dun Hill; Grains Moss; Laddow Rocks; Crowden (A628); Torside Reservoir; Wildboar Clough; Bleaklow Head; Wain Stones; Alport Low; Devil's Dike; Snake Pass Road A57); Featherbed Top; Upper Gate Clough; Ashop Clough (Snake Path); Black Ashop Edge; Kinder Scout plateau; Grindsbrook – EDALE (Old Nag's Head Inn).

The Kinder Round

ALTHOUGH this is a relatively low-level walk, it should not be underestimated; the Kinder Round is a demanding 25 mile circuit, requiring a good deal of commitment. The whole of the walk is covered by the Dark Peak map. Starting and finishing at Edale, the route is usually followed in an anti-clockwise direction:

EDALE (Fieldhead); Ollerbrook Booth; Nether Booth; Rowland Cote; Clough Farm; Jagger's Clough; Crookstone Barn; Blackley Clough; Upper Ashop; River Ashop; Snake Road(A57); Alport Bridge; Hayridge Farm; Oyster Clough; Dinas Sitch Tor; Snake Pass Inn; Ashop Clough (Snake Path); Ashop Head; William Clough; White Brow; Kinder Reservoir; Kinder Bank; Coldwell Clough; Kinderlow end; Stony Ford; Edale Cross; Jacob's Ladder; Lee Estate; Upper Booth – EDALE.

The Bleaklow Round

WEIGHING in at a mere twenty miles, this particular round-walk barely qualifies as long distance; but Bleaklow must never be underestimated. In bad weather the hill can become a monster, and even on a good day the trip demands stamina and confidence in map interpretation and compass techniques. The Dark Peak Map is the only one you will need, and the circular route – open to variation, of course – is (clockwise):

SNAKE PASS INN; Birchin Clough Bridge (A57); Birchin Clough; Over Wood Moss; Hern Clough; Wain Stones; Bleaklow Head; Bleaklow Hill; Bleaklow Stones; Grinah Stones; Barrow Stones; River Derwent; Slippery Stones; Howden Reservoir (west side); West End; Alport Castles; Alport Castles Farm; Hayridge Farm; Doctor's Gate; Snake Road (A57); SNAKE PASS INN.

The Derwent Watershed

EUSTACE Thomas's original forty mile circular walk still rates as the real test for bogtrotters. As with the Marsden-Edale, the route can be spread over two days; but to complete the route in a long day will be the goal of the reasonably fit and very determined rambler. The Dark Peak map covers most of the area, but the OS Sheet Number 110 (Sheffield & Huddersfield) 1:50 000 is necessary for planning the walk. The route is as follows, starting and finishing at the 'Yorkshire Bridge', Bamford, and travelling in a clockwise direction:

BAMFORD (Yorkshire Bridge); Parkin Clough; Win Hill; Lose Hill; Hollins Cross; Mam Tor; Rushup Edge; Horsehill Tor; Brown Knoll; Kinder Low; Kinder Downfall; Mill Hill; Moss Castle; Featherbed Moss; Snake Pass (A57); Devil's Dike; Wain Stones; Bleaklow Head; Bleaklow Hill; Bleaklow Stones; Swains Greave; Swains Head; Howden Edge; Crow Stones Edge; Margery Hill; Featherbed Moss; Back Tor; Derwent Edge; White Tor; Moscar (A57); Stanage End; Stanage Edge; High Neb; Bamford Edge; BAMFORD (Yorkshire Bridge).

The Three Inns

THE forty-mile Three Inns walk inaugurated by Fred Heardman, Donald Berwick and H.E. Wild in 1922 has been further developed into the Four Inns (to include the Old Nag's Head, Edale), and the Five Inns (to include the Flouch Inn, near Langsett) and so on. The Four Inns Walk which has become a regular competition for Scouts starts at Holmebridge and finishes at Harpur Hill, Buxton, but several variations are possible. The original route – for which you will need the OS Sheet Number 110 (Sheffield & Huddersfield) 1:50 000; OS Sheet Number 119 (Buxton, Matlock & Dovedale) 1: 50 000; and the Dark Peak map – started at Whaley Bridge and finished at Marsden. Plan your own route from the bare bones:

WHALEY BRIDGE; Cat & Fiddle Inn; Kinder Scout; Snake Pass Inn; Bleaklow; Crowden; Black Hill; Isle of Skye Inn (site of); MARSDEN.

SECTION C:
BACKGROUND FOR
BOGTROTTERS

FURTHER INFORMATION

Getting there..

The Peak National Park Authority is well aware of the fact that transport policy has long been on an environmentally unsustainable track. The problems of traffic congestion – with villages becoming grid-locked at times – and pollution demand immediate action. Some recent (1994)proposals are: an extension of the Park & Ride mini-bus scheme employed in the Goyt and Upper Derwent Valley (although road-closure is usually fiercely resisted by local business and residents); restraining private transport by limiting car-parking provisions; and the improvement of public transport within the Peak National Park. The Peak Park Planning Board provides funding from its severely limited resources for certain 'Mainline' bus services and a 'Green Way' railway service through the Hope Valley.

Up-to date timetables and maps of bus and train services can be found in the highly convenient Peak District Timetable Book, which may be obtained from bus stations, Information Centres and some Public Libraries in Derbyshire; or write to The Public Transport Unit, Derbyshire County Council, Chatsworth Hall, Matlock, Derbyshire, DE4 9BR.

..& staying there

An updated list of camping and caravan sites is published each year by the Peak National Park Board, and an Accommodation and Catering leaflet is also available. For information on local Youth Hostels, write to: YHA Peak Area Office, PO Box 11, Unit 5, Torr Mill, Dimple Road, Matlock, Derbyshire DE6 3JX.

ORGANISATIONS & ADDRESSES

PEAK NATIONAL PARK:
Aldern House, Baslow Road, BAKEWELL, Derbyshire DE45 1AE; Telephone Bakewell (0629) 814321.

For details of public transport, accommodation, and, indeed, anything you need to know about the Peak National Park, the **Information Centres** provide an excellent source. The following are based in the Dark Peak region:

EDALE (Fieldhead) – Telephone: Hope Valley (0433) 670207.

CASTLETON (Castle Street) – Telephone: 0433 620679.

UPPER DERWENT VALLEY (Fairholmes) – Telephone: 0433 650953.

LANGSETT (Langsett Barn) – Telephone: 0226 370770.

GLOSSOP (Norfolk Street) – Telephone: 0457 855920.

Other organisations that are of potential interest include:

THE NATIONAL TRUST, St. Anne's Gate, LONDON SW1;

NATIONAL TRUST REGIONAL OFFICE (East Midlands):
Clumber Park Stableyard, Worksop, Nottinghamshire S80 3BE

NATIONAL TRUST ESTATE OFFICE:
Edale End, Edale Road, Hope via SHEFFIELD. Telephone: Hope Valley (0433) 670368.

COUNCIL FOR THE PROTECTION OF RURAL ENGLAND:
Warwick House, 25 Buckingham Palace Road, London SW1W OPP. Telephone: 071-976 6433

THE RAMBLERS ASSOCIATION:
1/5 Wandsworth Road, London SW8 2XX. Telephone: 071 582 6878.

YOUTH HOSTELS ASSOCIATION (England & Wales):
National Office: Trevelyan House, 8 St. Stephen's Hill, St. Albans, Hertford-
shire AL1 2DY. Telephone: 0727 45047.

BRITISH MOUNTAINEERING COUNCIL:
Crawford House, Precinct Centre, Booth Street East, Manchester M13 9RZ.

LONG DISTANCE WALKERS ASSOCIATION:
Membership Secretary, Lodgefield Cottage, High Street, Flimwell, East
Sussex.

ROYAL SOCIETY FOR THE PROTECTION OF BIRDS:
The Lodge, Sandy, Bedfordshire SG19 2DL. Telephone: 0767 80551

THE FRIENDS OF NATIONAL PARKS:
246 Lavender Hill, London SW11 1LJ. Telephone: 071 924 4077

BIBLIOGRAPHY

Freedom To Roam: Howard Hill (Moorland,1980)

High Peak: Eric Byne & Geoffrey Sutton (Secker & Warburg, 1966)

On Foot In The Peak: Patrick Monkhouse (Alexander Maclehouse, 1932). Condensed photo-print edition published in 1988, with a foreword by Jim Perrin, by Diadem: *On Foot In North Wales and The Peak*.

The Peak and Pennines: W.A. Poucher (Constable, 1978)

Dark Peak Aircraft Wrecks (1&2): Ron Collier (Wharncliffe 1982; revised and expanded 1992 published by Leo Cooper, a division of Pen & Sword Books.)

Mountain Navigation: Peter Cliff (2nd ed., Cordee, 1980)

Mountain Navigation Techniques: Kevin Walker (Constable, 1986)

Mountain Weather: David Pedgley (Cicerone Press, 1979)

Safety On Mountains: British Mountaineering Council

Birds by Character: the field guide to jizz identification – Hume, Wallace, Rees, Busby & Partington (Macmillan)

Consult *High*, *The Great Outdoors* and *Climber & Hillwalker* magazines for up-to-the-minute information.

We publish a wide range of other titles, including general interest publications, guides to individual towns, and books for outdoor activities centred on walking and cycling in the great outdoors throughout England and Wales. This is a recent selection:

Peak District Walks

HERITAGE WALKS IN THE PEAK DISTRICT - Clive Price *(£6.95)*

CHALLENGING WALKS IN NORTH-WEST BRITAIN - Ron Astley *(£7.95)*

WALKING PEAKLAND TRACKWAYS - Mike Cresswell *(£7.95)*

MOSTLY DOWNHILL, Leisurely Walks - White Peak - Clive Price *(£6.95)*

MOSTLY DOWNHILL, Leisurely Walks - Dark Peak - Clive Price *(£6.95)*

Cycling with Sigma

CYCLE UK! The Essential Guide to Leisure Cycling
- Les Lumsdon *(£9.95)*

OFF-BEAT CYCLING & MOUNTAIN BIKING IN THE PEAK DISTRICT
- Clive Smith *(£6.95)*

MORE OFF-BEAT CYCLING IN THE PEAK DISTRICT
- Clive Smith *(£6.95)*

50 BEST CYCLE RIDES IN CHESHIRE
- edited by Graham Beech *(£7.95)*

CYCLING IN THE LAKE DISTRICT
- John Wood *(£7.95)*

CYCLING IN SOUTH WALES
- Rosemary Evans *(£7.95)*

CYCLING IN THE COTSWOLDS
- Stephen Hill *(£7.95)*

BY-WAY BIKING IN THE CHILTERNS
- Henry Tindell *(£7.95)*

Country Walking . . .

RAMBLES IN NORTH WALES - Roger Redfern

EAST CHESHIRE WALKS - Graham Beech

WEST CHESHIRE WALKS - Jen Darling

WEST PENNINE WALKS - Mike Cresswell

STAFFORDSHIRE WALKS - Les Lumsdon

NEWARK AND SHERWOOD RAMBLES - Malcolm McKenzie

NORTH NOTTINGHAMSHIRE RAMBLES - Malcolm McKenzie

RAMBLES AROUND NOTTINGHAM & DERBY - Keith Taylor

RAMBLES AROUND MANCHESTER - Mike Cresswell

WESTERN LAKELAND RAMBLES - Gordon Brown *(£5.95)*

WELSH WALKS: Dolgellau and the Cambrian Coast
- Laurence Main and Morag Perrott *(£5.95)*

WELSH WALKS: Aberystwyth and District
- Laurence Main and Morag Perrott *(£5.95)*

WEST PENNINE WALKS - Mike Cresswell

MOSTLY DOWNHILL, Leisurely Walks in the Lake District - Clive Price

- all of the above books are currently £6.95 each, except where indicated

Long-distance walks:

THE GREATER MANCHESTER BOUNDARY WALK - Graham Phythian

THE THIRLMERE WAY - Tim Cappelli

THE FURNESS TRAIL - Tim Cappelli

THE MARCHES WAY - Les Lumsdon

THE TWO ROSES WAY - Peter Billington, Eric Slater, Bill Greenwood and
Clive Edwards

THE RED ROSE WALK - Tom Schofield

FROM WHARFEDALE TO WESTMORLAND:
historical walks through the Yorkshire Dales - Aline Watson

THE WEST YORKSHIRE WAY - Nicholas Parrott

- all £6.95 each

The Best Pub Walks!

Sigma publish the widest range of "Pub Walks" guides, covering just about every popular walking destination in England and Wales. Each book includes 25 - 30 interesting walks and varied suitable for individuals or family groups. *The walks are based on "Real Ale" inns of character and are all accessible by public transport.*

Areas covered include

Cheshire • Dartmoor • Exmoor • Isle of Wight • Yorkshire Dales • Peak District • Lake District • Cotswolds • Mendips • Cornwall • Lancashire • Oxfordshire • Snowdonia • Devon • Northumbria • Snowdonia • Manchester

… and dozens more - all £6.95 each!

General interest:

THE INCREDIBLY BIASED BEER GUIDE - Ruth Herman
This is the most comprehensive guide to Britain's smaller breweries and the pubs where you can sample their products. Produced with the collaboration of the Small Independent Brewers' Association and including a half-price subscription to The Beer Lovers' Club. *£6.95*

DIAL 999 - EMERGENCY SERVICES IN ACTION - John Creighton
Re-live the excitement as fire engines rush to disasters. See dramatic rescues on land and sea. Read how the professionals keep a clear head and swing into action. **£6.95**

THE ALABAMA AFFAIR - David Hollett
This is an account of Britain's rôle in the American Civil War. Read how Merseyside dockyards supplied ships for the Confederate navy, thereby supporting the slave trade. The *Alabama* was the most famous of the 'Laird Rams', and was chased half way across the world before being sunk ignominiously. *£6.95*

PEAK DISTRICT DIARY - Roger Redfern
An evocative book, celebrating the glorious countryside of the Peak District. The book is based on Roger's popular column in *The Guardian* newspaper and is profusely illustrated with stunning photographs. *£6.95*

I REMAIN, YOUR SON JACK - J. C. Morten (edited by Sheila Morten)
A collection of almost 200 letters, as featured on BBC TV, telling the moving story of a young soldier in the First World War. Profusely illustrated with contemporary photographs. *£8.95*

FORGOTTEN DIVISIONS - John Fox
A unique account of the 1914 - 18 War, drawing on the experience of soldiers and civilians, from a Lancashire town and a Rhineland village. The book is well illustrated and contains many unique photographs. *£7.95*

ROAD SENSE - Doug Holland

A book for drivers with some experience, preparing them for an advanced driving test. The book introduces a recommended system of car control, based on that developed by the Police Driving School. Doug Holland is a highly qualified driving instructor, working with RoSPA. *£5.95*

TRAINING THE LEARNER DRIVER - Don Gates

The essential guide for all those intending to teach a friend or relation to drive. Written by a drivng professional so that you'll know that you are teaching just the same way as a driving instructor. £6.95

WE ALSO PUBLISH:

A new series of investigations into the Supernatural, Myth and Magic:

GHOSTS, TRADITIONS AND LEGENDS OF OLD LANCASHIRE
- Ken Howarth *(£7.95)*

SHADOWS: A northern investigation of the unknown
- Steve Cliffe *(£7.95)*

MYSTERIES OF THE MERSEY VALLEY
- Jenny Randles and Peter Hough *(£7.95)*

Plus, superb illustrated books on Manchester's football teams:

RED FEVER! From Rochdale to Rio as United Supporters *(£7.95)*

MANCHESTER UNITED - Moments to Remember *(£6.95)*

MANCHESTER CITY - Moments to Remember *(£9.95)*

Many more entertaining and educational books are being regularly added to our list. All of our books are available from your local bookshop. In case of difficulty, or to obtain our complete catalogue, please contact:

Sigma Leisure,
1 South Oak Lane, Wilmslow, Cheshire SK9 6AR

Phone: 0625 - 531035 Fax: 0625 - 536800

ACCESS and VISA orders welcome - call our friendly sales staff or use our 24 hour Answerphone service! Most orders are despatched on the day we receive your order - you could be enjoying our books in just a couple of days.